Contents

II   Ideas List

Preface

Welcome to *101 Business Ideas for Kids*! This book is your go-to guide for learning how to start your very own business—no matter your age or experience. Whether you've already got an idea or have no clue where to start, you're in the right place.

This book is divided into two helpful parts:

Part 1 (the first 19 chapters) gives you the tools and knowledge to actually build and run a business. You'll learn how to come up with ideas, talk to customers, make a logo, create a website, and more. It's like a crash course in entrepreneurship—just for kids!

Part 2 is packed with 108 real business ideas you can explore right now. From lemonade stands to digital art shops to tech help for seniors, these ideas are designed to spark your creativity and help you find something you'll love.

You don't have to be perfect. You don't have to know everything. You just have to be willing to start. Let this book be your launchpad. Ready? Let's go!

I

Part One

Chapters 1–19: How to Build Your Business from Scratch
In this section, you'll learn the basics of how to become an entrepreneur. From finding the right idea to building a brand, making a logo, talking to customers, and even keeping track of money—you'll get step-by-step guidance to start your own small business. These chapters are fun, easy to follow, and full of real tools and tips to help turn your idea into something real.

Chapter 1: What Is a Business?

Have you ever sold slime to your friends? Thought about making money from your drawings? Or offered to mow your neighbor's lawn for a few bucks?

If so — you've already started thinking like an entrepreneur.

So what *is* a business, really?

At its simplest, a business is something that makes money by selling something — a **product**, a **service**, or even a **digital product** like a graphic, a song, or a gaming skin. It's a way to take something you create or something you can do, and offer it to people who want it.

That might sound serious or complicated, but it's not. A business can be as small as a lemonade stand or as big as Amazon. The size doesn't matter — what matters is the **value** you're offering and how you share it with others.

What Can a Business Sell?

Most businesses sell one (or more) of the following:

1. **Physical Products** – These are things you can touch, hold, or use. Cookies, bracelets, lip balm, stickers, T-shirts, candles, phone stands — if you can package it and hand it to someone, it's a physical product.
2. **Services** – These are things you *do* for people. Pet-sitting, tu-

toring, lawn care, washing cars, helping someone organize their closet — if you're helping solve a problem by doing something for someone else, you're offering a service.

3. **Digital Products** – These live online. Maybe you sell graphic designs, printable planners, Minecraft skins, coding tutorials, or eBooks. Once they're made, digital products can be downloaded or shared instantly — no shipping required.

Some of the coolest kid businesses actually combine categories. Imagine designing logos (digital), printing them on shirts (physical), and delivering them locally (service). That's a real business — and you could start something like that, too.

Why Do People Pay?

People pay money to make their life easier, better, cooler, or more fun.

That's really it.

Think about it:

- Someone's hungry? They buy food.
- They want to laugh? They pay for a movie or a meme page.
- They want their dog walked while they're at work? That's a service they'll happily pay for.
- They want to look professional at work? They buy sharp-looking scrubs or a new lab coat.
- They need help remembering their homework? They download a planner or digital calendar.
- They want their YouTube channel to look cool? They buy a banner or thumbnail design.
- They need a gift for a friend? They buy a handmade bracelet or custom digital artwork.

- They want to learn how to draw anime? They buy a digital tutorial or sign up for a class.
- They want to protect their phone? They buy a case from a kid-owned brand with fun colors.
- They want to feel good about supporting someone their age? They buy from a small kid-run business!

You don't have to invent the next iPhone. Just think about what people *already want* — and how you can offer it better, faster, cheaper, or in a more fun or personal way.

Look Around You

Now pause. Wherever you're reading this — your bedroom, the kitchen, a classroom — look around.

Unless you're sitting outside in a forest, nearly *everything* you see came from a business.

Your chair? Business.

The hoodie you're wearing? Business.

The snack in your hand? Business.

The app on your phone? Business again.

Every item, every logo, every website — all of it started with an idea that someone turned into a business. And those "someones" weren't all adults in suits. Some of them were teens, kids, or students just like you.

Business is everywhere — and you're surrounded by it.

What Every Business Needs

You don't have to memorize this list, but here's a quick look at the building blocks most businesses share:

- **An idea** – Something people want or need.
- **Something to sell** – A product, service, or digital item.

- **Customers** – People willing to pay.
- **A way to deliver** – A website, a store, a text message — just a way to get it to them.
- **A way to get paid** – Cash, Venmo, PayPal, a website with checkout.

You don't need permission to start. You don't need a fancy plan or a huge loan. You just need to take the first step.

You Might Already Be Closer Than You Think

If you've ever:

- Traded cards or collectibles
- Baked something and sold it at school or a party
- Offered to help neighbors or family for a few bucks
- Thought, *"Why doesn't someone sell this?"*

...you're already thinking like an entrepreneur.

This book will help you go from "thinking" to "doing."

It's okay to be nervous. It's okay to start small. But don't underestimate what you're capable of. Some of the world's biggest companies started in basements, bedrooms, and garages.

Yours could, too.

So let's get going — because your business starts right now.

Chapter 2: Why Start a Business?

Let's say someone handed you $100.

Would you spend it? Save it? Use some for snacks and some for that one thing sitting in your online cart?

Now imagine if *you* earned that $100 yourself — through your own creativity, time, and effort.

It would feel different, right?

That's one of the coolest things about starting a business: it gives you the power to create something out of nothing. Whether it's $5 or $5,000, when it's your money, it *means* something.

But here's the secret: starting a business isn't just about making money. It's about freedom. It's about creativity. It's about building something that's yours.

Let's talk about why you might want to start a business — even if you're still "just a kid."

🔘 Reason #1: You Can Make Your Own Money

Let's start with the obvious one: money.

When you start a business, you're not waiting for allowance or asking your parents for extra cash. You're creating your *own* source of income — and that feels amazing.

You can use that money however you want:

- Save up for a bike, game system, or phone
- Treat yourself to snacks or fun stuff
- Buy gifts for family or friends
- Reinvest into your business to make even more

You're in control. You're the boss. That's a pretty awesome feeling.

🎨 Reason #2: You Get to Be Creative

Businesses are built on ideas. *Your* ideas.

You might design stickers, come up with a funny brand name, build a website, create content, or invent something totally new. Every decision — from colors to packaging to how you talk to customers — is up to you.

Your business is a way to express yourself. It's your creative playground, and the best part? There are no rules (well, okay... some rules, but you get the idea).

Reason #3: It Teaches You Independence

When you run a business, you don't have to wait for someone to tell you what to do.

You decide:

- What to sell
- How much to charge
- When to work
- How to grow

Sure, you might ask for help along the way (and that's smart!), but the business is *yours*. You don't have to be an adult to take charge of something big.

That feeling of independence — knowing you made something real happen — is one of the most powerful parts of being an entrepreneur.

✊ Reason #4: It Builds Confidence

Starting a business can be scary. What if it doesn't work? What if nobody buys?

Here's the truth: even trying builds courage.

Every step — from naming your business to selling your first product — helps you believe in yourself more.

You'll get better at talking to people, solving problems, and trusting your instincts. You'll start to think, *"If I can do this, what else can I do?"*

That's real confidence, and you earn it by doing.

🕵 Reason #5: You Learn Real-World Skills

Starting a business teaches you stuff that school usually doesn't. Things like:

- How to manage money
- How to market and promote your ideas
- How to deal with customers (even the tricky ones)
- How to set goals and stay organized
- How to use tools like spreadsheets, design apps, and websites

These are grown-up skills — and you're learning them early. Whether you run a business forever or not, these skills will help you in school, in jobs, and throughout life.

👶 Reason #6: You Don't Have to Wait to Be a Grown-Up

There's no age limit to starting a business. Some of the world's most successful entrepreneurs started young.

Here are just a few real examples:

- **Mikaila Ulmer** started selling lemonade with honey at age 4 — and turned it into *Me & the Bees Lemonade*, a brand now sold in major grocery stores.
- **Moziah Bridges** began sewing bow ties when he was 9. Now, *Mo's Bows* has been featured on Shark Tank and in fashion magazines.
- **Alina Morse** was just 7 when she created *Zolli Candy*, a sugar-free candy that's now sold in Walmart and CVS.

What do they all have in common? They didn't wait. They saw an opportunity and went for it.

You can, too.

⊙ Reason #7: You Can Make an Impact

Some businesses are just for fun. Some are about solving problems. But many businesses also make the world better.

You could:

- Raise money for a cause you care about
- Help people in your neighborhood
- Support the environment by using recycled materials
- Make others feel included, seen, or celebrated

Your business doesn't just have to earn money — it can do good, too.

📖 Final Thought

You don't have to be rich. You don't have to be perfect. You don't need a fancy office or a grown-up title.

All you need is an idea and the courage to try.

Even if your first business is small — a few customers, a few dollars — it teaches you BIG lessons. Lessons about people, money, effort, and yourself.

And once you learn how to build something from scratch, you'll never forget that feeling.

That's why we start.

That's why it matters.

That's why you can do it.

Let's get to work.

Chapter 3: Who Starts Businesses?

What do a gamer, a dog walker, a baker, and a 13-year-old who loves editing videos all have in common?

They can all start businesses.

One of the coolest things about being an entrepreneur is that there's **no one "type" of person** who starts a business. You don't need to wear a suit. You don't have to have a huge following. And you definitely don't need to wait until you're a grown-up.

In fact, some of the most creative and successful businesses today are being started by *young people*, from *all over the world*, in all kinds of ways.

🌍 Anyone Can Do It — From Anywhere

A long time ago, starting a business usually meant having a store, a lot of money, and a physical location. But now? Thanks to computers, phones, and the internet, you can run a business **from almost anywhere** — your bedroom, your kitchen table, or even your school library.

You can design logos in Florida and sell them to people in London.

You can write eBooks in Kenya and upload them to Amazon in seconds.

You can bake cookies in your neighborhood and promote them on Instagram.

Geography doesn't matter as much anymore. You don't have to live in a big city. You don't need to be famous. If you've got Wi-Fi and an idea, you've already got a head start.

👥 You Don't Have to Be a "Business Person"

A lot of people think business owners have to be a certain type:

- Super confident
- Good at math
- Always talking in meetings
- Wearing suits and carrying briefcases

Nope.

Some entrepreneurs are quiet and thoughtful.

Some love art and hate spreadsheets.

Some are introverts who'd rather create something amazing than give a big speech.

And guess what? That's all totally okay.

Your personality doesn't limit you — it's actually your *superpower*. The way you think, create, and connect with others is exactly what makes your business *uniquely yours*.

⭐ Real Examples of Young Entrepreneurs (That You May Not Know Yet)

Let's check out some real kids and teens who started businesses by being themselves:

- **Neha Gupta** (started at age 9) began selling handmade crafts and holding fundraising events to help orphans in India. Her business turned into a nonprofit that's helped thousands of kids get access to education.

- **Ryan Hickman** (age 10) started *Ryan's Recycling* in California by collecting bottles and cans from neighbors. He's recycled over 1 million bottles — and built a brand with eco-friendly merch and outreach.
- **Lily Born** was just 12 when she invented the *Kangaroo Cup*, a spill-proof cup for people with motor challenges, like her grandfather. Now it's sold worldwide.
- **Zoe Oli** started a doll company at age 6 because she didn't see enough dolls that looked like her. Today, *Beautiful Curly Me* sells dolls, books, and hair care kits, inspiring girls everywhere.

None of these kids followed the same path. They saw something they cared about — and they turned it into a business.

Different Passions, Different Paths

Not every business has to be about making a million dollars. Some are just about doing something you *love* and sharing it with others.

Let's say you:

- Love organizing? You could help neighbors clean their garages.
- Love gaming? You could create tutorials, design skins, or host events.
- Love animals? You could offer pet-sitting, dog-walking, or treat-baking.
- Love drawing? You could sell art, stickers, or digital wallpapers.
- Love helping people? You could tutor kids in subjects you're great at.

There's no single "right" kind of business. What matters is finding something *you're into* — and figuring out how it could help others or make them smile.

✧ You Can Be Different — That's the Point

Maybe you live in a small town.

Maybe you're homeschooled.

Maybe you don't know anyone else who's ever started a business.

Maybe you've never even thought of yourself as a "leader."

Guess what? That's all okay.

In fact, some of the best businesses are started by people who *don't* fit the mold. People who bring a new point of view. People who notice something others missed.

That might be you.

◉ Final Thought

You don't have to wait.

You don't have to be someone else.

You don't have to move to a big city, be the loudest in the room, or know every answer.

You just have to start.

Because the truth is: *anyone* can start a business — and that includes you.

Chapter 4: What Makes a Business Succeed?

Have you ever seen someone trying to sell something... and no one's interested? Then someone else offers the *same* thing — and suddenly, everyone's lining up?

What's the difference?

It's not always the product. It's often about *how* the business works — how it's shared, how it's delivered, how it's improved, and how much effort the person behind it puts in.

So what makes one business succeed while another one struggles? Let's break it down.

✔ Success Starts with Solving a Problem *and/or* Creating Joy

A great business helps people in some way. That help might come from solving a problem — or from offering something fun, exciting, or cool.

Some examples:

- A pet-sitting service solves the problem of busy families needing help with their pets.
- A kid who sells custom hoodies is creating something fun and stylish.
- A homemade brownie business solves the "I'm hungry" problem

and brings happiness with every bite.

Many of the best businesses do both — they fix something and make people feel good doing it.

So when you're thinking about your business idea, ask yourself:

"Does this help someone in some way — or make their life a little better or more fun?"

If the answer is yes, you're off to a strong start.

⇔ Listen and Improve: The Feedback Loop

Even a great idea can flop if you don't listen.

Smart entrepreneurs always pay attention to how people respond to their product or service. Did they love it? Was something confusing? Would they buy it again?

This is called a **feedback loop**, and it works like this:

1. Try something
2. See how people respond
3. Make improvements
4. Try again

It's like leveling up a video game character — but you're leveling up your business instead.

The best businesses are *always* evolving. They update their packaging, tweak their pricing, try new versions, or add helpful features — all based on what they learn from real customers.

So don't take feedback personally. Use it to grow stronger.

⧗ Show Up and Keep Going

Success doesn't happen overnight. You might only get one order the first week. Maybe your first customer is your grandma (hey, that still counts!).

But showing up again and again — creating, selling, listening, improving — that's where the magic happens.

Every popular business you see today? It started with a small beginning. A single sale. A single post. A single person saying, *"Let's try this."*

Stick with it. Keep showing up.

🎁 Deliver What You Promise

If someone buys something from you, they're trusting you.

Your job is to follow through:

- Deliver the product when you said you would
- Make it as awesome as you promised
- Be kind, respectful, and honest in how you communicate

Even if you make a mistake (which happens!), owning it and making it right builds **trust** — and trust is the secret to getting people to come back.

Customers don't need perfection. They need reliability.

📖 Keep Learning

Here's a secret: even adults don't know everything about business. They're still learning, experimenting, and improving — just like you.

Whether you're selling bracelets or building a YouTube editing business, always keep learning:

- Watch tutorials
- Read blogs
- Ask other entrepreneurs questions
- Learn from mistakes instead of being embarrassed by them

Every mistake is a step forward if you learn from it.

💪 Success Takes Hard Work

Let's be real: running a business isn't easy.

Sometimes things go wrong. Sometimes you feel tired. Sometimes nobody buys — even when you try your best.

That's where one of the most important ingredients for success comes in: **hard work**.

You have to be willing to:

- Keep going when it's not exciting
- Try again when something fails
- Push through when it gets hard or slow

Successful entrepreneurs are **relentless** — they don't give up just because something didn't work on the first try. They figure out a new way, fix what's broken, and keep moving forward.

If you're willing to work hard, you're already ahead of most people.

⦿ Final Thought

Success in business isn't about being lucky or super smart. It's about:

- Helping people
- Listening and improving
- Delivering what you promise
- Working hard
- And sticking with it when others would quit

You don't need permission. You don't need perfection. You just need to care, try, and keep going. But it obviously helps if you can build a better mouse trap or find a new improved way of doing something in this world that people value.

If you do that? You've already got what it takes.

Chapter 5: How to Pick the Right Idea for You

Let's get this out of the way early: there's no such thing as a perfect idea.

Some of the best businesses start from small, simple ideas — ideas that match the person running them. That's what this chapter is about: figuring out what kind of business might be the right fit for **you**.

Not your friend. Not your favorite YouTuber.

You.

💡 Start with What You Like

If you could spend a free Saturday doing anything — what would you choose?

Drawing? Baking? Organizing your closet? Gaming? Filming videos? Helping people?

Your hobbies and interests are a great place to begin. Why? Because starting a business takes energy, and it's a lot easier to stick with something you actually enjoy.

For example:

- Love dogs? You could start a pet-sitting or treat-baking business.
- Into art? You could sell custom drawings, stickers, or phone backgrounds.

- Obsessed with shoes? Maybe you clean, resell, or customize sneakers.
- Enjoy Minecraft? You could build maps, host events, or make tutorials.

The point is: you already have passions. Let's build from there.

🌑 What Are You Good At (or Want to Get Good At)?

Think about what comes naturally to you — or something you're curious to learn.

Are you good at explaining things? You might be a great tutor or content creator.

Are you super organized? You could help people clean or plan.

Do you have an eye for color or design? That's useful for logos, websites, or crafts.

And if you're thinking, *"But I'm not good at anything yet..."* — that's totally fine. You don't need to be a pro. The best entrepreneurs start with an interest and grow their skills along the way.

All you need is:

1. Something you enjoy
2. A willingness to learn
3. The courage to try

That's enough.

👀 What Do People Around You Need or Want?

This is where businesses come to life.

Think about the people around you — your friends, family, classmates, neighbors, teachers. What do they struggle with? What would make their life easier? What do they buy often?

Some examples:

- Do your neighbors work a lot? Maybe they need help with pets, packages, or plants.
- Do your classmates love cool school supplies? You could make custom notebooks or locker decorations.
- Does your community love sports? Sell fan gear, team snacks, or tournament posters.
- Do people around you own small businesses? Offer to help with social media, flyers, or product photos.

The best business ideas often connect what *you* love with what *someone else* needs.

⏲ Time, Tools, and Limits

Now let's get real: What can you actually do with what you've got? Ask yourself:

- How much time do I really have each week?
- Do I have access to a kitchen, computer, art supplies, or a phone?
- Will my parents or guardians be able to help with any part of this?

It's okay if your time or tools are limited — many great businesses started with just paper, scissors, and glue. The goal is to pick something **realistic** for your current situation.

Later on, you can always grow.

Test Small First

Here's a powerful business secret: **start small**.

Before you build a whole website or print 100 products, try a tiny version of your idea. Sell one item. Offer your service to one customer.

Test it with a family member or neighbor.
Ask:

- Did they like it?
- What would they change?
- Would they pay for it again?

This gives you real feedback without wasting time, money, or energy. Starting small also gives you a confidence boost — because once someone says yes, it suddenly feels *real*.

⚡ Your Idea Might Change — That's Okay!
You're not locking yourself into this one idea forever.
Many of the world's best businesses started as something else:

- YouTube started as a dating site (!)
- Nintendo began as a playing card company
- Instagram was originally a check-in app like Foursquare

The key is to *start somewhere*. As you learn what works (and what doesn't), you can always adjust.
You're not stuck — you're just starting.

◉ Final Thought
The best idea for you is one that:

- You actually enjoy
- You're excited to learn about
- You can start with the time and tools you already have
- Other people might find helpful, fun, or cool

Don't stress about finding the "perfect" idea.

Just pick something small that feels exciting — and take the first step. You'll figure out the rest along the way.

Chapter 6: What Type of Business Should I Start?

Selling cookies. Designing a custom app. Walking your neighbor's dog.

These are all real businesses — but they work in very different ways.

Before you jump into your big idea, it helps to understand the **three main types of businesses** you can start: physical product businesses, digital product businesses, and service-based businesses. Each one has different strengths, challenges, and tools — and the best choice depends on what fits *you*.

Let's break them down.

Physical Product Businesses

What it is: You sell something physical — something people can touch, hold, or use.

Examples: Slime, bracelets, baked goods, t-shirts, candles, stickers, or even **a widget or gadget you invent** to solve a specific problem.

🔥 **Pros:**

- Fun to make and sell
- Easy for people to understand — "I give you money, you give me the product"
- If people love it, you can scale quickly and make more money as

you sell more

⚠ Challenges:

- You usually need to **buy or make inventory**
- If you're producing your own product:
- You might be able to make it at home with your family or friends
- But if it grows, you may need to work with a **factory** to produce larger batches
- You might have to **pay upfront** for supplies or bulk orders
- You need a place to store your products
- You have to deliver or ship items to customers
- If you work with a manufacturer in another country (like China, Mexico, or India), you'll need to learn about **importing, shipping times, and quality control**
- One alternative is **dropshipping**, where you sell a product online, and a third-party company makes and ships it for you. It's lower risk, but you make less money and have less control over quality

Great for you if:

You enjoy hands-on work, love making things, and are ready to handle (or learn about) packaging, shipping, or inventory.

🖥 Digital Product Businesses

What it is: You create something digital — something people download, use online, or access through a device.

Examples: Art files, gaming templates, printable planners, eBooks, music, digital birthday invitations, or YouTube overlays.

Once you make it, you can sell it to many people over and over without having to make it again.

✎ Special Focus: Software & Apps

Yes, even kids can create **apps or software tools**!

Thanks to **no-code** platforms like **Thunkable, MIT App Inventor, Glide, or Scratch**, you can create:

- A to-do list app
- A simple game
- A calculator for classmates
- A journaling app
- Or even a quiz or study tool

You don't need to be a coding expert. Many tools are beginner-friendly and made for students.

✎ Pros:

- No physical inventory
- Can sell or share your product many times
- Huge potential to scale
- Great if you're creative, techy, or love designing

⚠ Challenges:

- You need computer or tablet access
- You might have to learn new tools or software
- Sometimes people don't "see" the product like they do with something physical, so you'll need to explain or show its value clearly

Great for you if:

You enjoy working with technology, want to create something once and sell it many times, and like designing, writing, or building online tools.

Service-Based Businesses

What it is: You help people by doing something useful for them.

Examples: Babysitting, tutoring, pet-sitting, dog walking, cleaning, car washing, organizing, running errands, or helping someone with their tech setup.

You don't sell a thing — you sell your time, your help, and your skills.

👍 **Pros:**

- No inventory or product supplies needed (for most services)
- Quick to start
- People are always looking for reliable helpers — especially if they trust you

⚠ **Challenges:**

- You trade **time for money,** so you can only help so many people at once
- It's harder to "scale" unless you raise prices or hire help
- You need to be dependable and good at working with others

Great for you if:

You like helping people, are organized and reliable, and want to start earning quickly using your time and effort.

? How Do You Choose?

Ask yourself:

- Do I like **making things, creating digital content,** or **helping others?**

- Do I have the time, space, or desire to store products or ship items?
- Do I prefer working online or in person?
- What fits into my life *right now* — school, family, and other activities?

There's no wrong answer. Just choose what fits your situation best — you can always pivot later.

⇔ Can I Combine Business Types?
Absolutely!

Let's say you make physical bookmarks — that's a **product**.

Then you offer a printable version — that's **digital**.

Then you help other kids design bookmarks for their businesses — that's a **service**.

Many of the best businesses combine all three. Once you start, you'll see how flexible things can be.

◉ Final Thought
Each type of business has its own pros and challenges. The right one for *you* is the one that:

- Fits your interests
- Matches your tools and time
- And gets you excited to start

Once you understand what kind of business you're building, you'll know how to plan it, grow it, and make it awesome.

Chapter 7: Should I Hire My Friends or Family?

So, your best friend wants to help with your business.

Your cousin has some great ideas.

Your sibling says they'll work for snacks.

Even your mom offers to be your "co-CEO."

It sounds fun, right?

But before you say "yes," there's something important to think about:

Working with friends or family *can* be awesome — or it can get really messy.

Let's talk about when it makes sense, what to watch out for, and how to protect both your business *and* your relationships.

☙ The Pros of Working with Friends or Family

There are some great things about teaming up with people you already know:

- You trust them.
- They're easy to talk to.
- You already have fun together.
- You might get extra help — like a parent who drives you to make deliveries, or a sibling who helps pack orders.

· It's less lonely to build something *together*.

Working with someone close to you can make your business feel like a team — not just a solo mission.

⚠ The Cons (and Cautions)
But here's the other side:

· **Not everyone takes it seriously.** Your friend might be excited at first... and then disappear when it's time to do the work.
· **It can get awkward.** If someone doesn't do their part, how do you bring it up without hurting their feelings?
· **Money changes things.** Who gets paid? How much? What if one person works harder than the other?
· **Family might take over.** Some adults mean well, but might try to take charge or make big decisions without asking you.
· **If things go wrong... it can damage your relationship.** That's a big deal. A business can be restarted — a friendship or family bond is harder to fix.

? Ask These Questions Before You Say "Yes"
Before you team up with someone, talk about it — for real.
Here are some questions to ask:

· Do I trust this person to actually show up and do the work?
· Are we both equally excited about this idea?
· Can we be honest with each other if something's not working?
· Are we okay with making decisions together — and sometimes disagreeing?
· What happens if one of us wants to quit?

If you can't talk through those questions, you probably shouldn't run a business together — at least not yet.

Talk About the End... Before You Start

This one's important — and most people skip it.

Even if things feel fun and exciting now, one of you might want to quit later.

That doesn't make them bad — it just means life changes.

Before you start, ask:

- What will we do if one person wants to stop?
- Does the business shut down?
- Can the other person keep it going alone?
- How will we split any money, supplies, or customers?

If this is just a quick summer project or a fun weekend hustle, no big deal.

But if you're starting something you want to grow over time, **make a plan for what happens if things don't go as planned.**

It's not being negative — it's being smart.

❤ Real Talk: You're Risking the Relationship

This might be the most important part of this chapter.

Starting a business with someone you care about always comes with a risk:

If it goes badly, you could lose the relationship.

That doesn't mean you *can't* do it. Plenty of families run amazing businesses together. Some best friends have built huge brands.

But it only works if:

- You're both mature enough to communicate clearly

- You can separate business stuff from personal stuff
- You both care more about the relationship than winning an argument

Before you say yes, ask yourself:

"Would I rather have this business... or this friendship?"

Sometimes, it's better to keep those two things separate.

✅ If You Do Work Together, Get Organized

If you decide to go for it, here's how to keep things running smoothly:

- Agree on who does what
- Write it down (even just in a notebook or shared Google Doc)
- Use a checklist, calendar, or shared to-do list
- Talk often — not just when something goes wrong
- Celebrate wins *together*

Clarity avoids most drama.

🙌 Tips for Working with Family

- Be respectful — especially if adults are helping you out
- Don't assume they'll always be available
- If they're doing favors (like driving or paying for supplies), thank them
- Let them know how much it means to you

Kindness goes a long way.

What If It Doesn't Work Out?

Sometimes, the partnership just doesn't work.

That's okay.

What matters is how you handle it:

· Talk honestly
· End things kindly
· Learn from it — what worked, what didn't, what you'd do differently next time

Business can end. Friendships and family should last longer.

⊚ Final Thought

Working with friends or family can be **amazing** — or **really tricky**. The key is to treat it like a *real* business: set expectations, plan ahead, and talk often.

Just remember: no business is worth losing someone you care about.

If you're going to team up, protect the relationship *first* — and build the business *second*.

That's how real entrepreneurs — and great friends — do it.

Chapter 8: How to Set Goals for Your Business

So... what's your goal?

Do you want to make your first $50?

Sell 20 bracelets?

Gain 10 new customers?

Start a YouTube channel and get 1,000 views?

No matter what your business idea is, **you need a goal** — something specific you're trying to do. Without a goal, it's easy to get distracted or discouraged. With a goal, you stay focused and motivated.

Let's walk through how to set goals that actually help you grow — and how to keep track of them without making it complicated.

⊙ Why Goals Matter

Goals help you know where you're going. They give you a reason to take action every day.

When you have a clear goal:

- You can stay focused even when things get busy or boring
- You can tell if your business is improving
- You know when to celebrate!

Here's a powerful saying from the business world:

"If you can't measure it, you can't manage it."

That means if you're not keeping track of something — even in a simple way — you can't improve it.

What Should You Measure?

Start with something **simple** and connected to what you do.

Here are a few examples of **trackable goals**:

- Sell 20 items this month
- Get 10 new email subscribers
- Knock on 5 doors each day to promote your service
- Post 3 times a week on social media
- Save $100 by the end of summer
- Hand out 50 flyers by the end of the weekend

Your goals don't need to be fancy — they just need to be **specific** and **countable**.

📅 Break It Down: Big Goals = Small Steps

Big goals can feel overwhelming — unless you break them into small pieces.

Let's say your goal is to earn $100 this month. That might seem big at first, but if you divide it up:

- That's $25 per week
- Or about $3.50 per day
- That might be one cookie sale... or one lawn mowed... or one digital download sold

Suddenly, it feels doable.

Breaking goals down makes them feel **real** — and gives you something to focus on each day or week.

✔ Use a Simple Tracker

Once you have a goal, find a fun and easy way to track your progress. You could use:

- A notebook
- A sticky note wall
- A printable chart
- A whiteboard
- An app on your phone (with your parent's permission)

Make it visual so you can **see** how far you've come. You could create a bar you fill in, cross off boxes, or color in a chart as you get closer to your goal.

It doesn't have to be perfect — it just has to help you stay focused.

⮂ Be Flexible — Goals Can Change

Sometimes you set a goal and realize halfway through:

- It's too hard right now
- It needs more time
- You picked the wrong thing to focus on

That's okay.

Real entrepreneurs change their goals all the time. What matters is that you **learn something** and keep going.

If you find that your goal isn't working, ask:

- Is this still the right goal for me?
- Can I break it down even more?

- Do I need to try a different strategy?

Adjusting a goal doesn't mean failing — it means improving.

🎉 Celebrate Your Wins

When you reach a goal — *celebrate!*
That might mean:

- Telling a friend or family member
- Doing a happy dance
- Taking a break to play your favorite game
- Writing it down in a notebook or journal
- Setting a new, bigger goal!

Celebrating makes you feel proud, and it reminds you that your effort is paying off.

Even small wins matter. They build confidence, momentum, and motivation.

🗣 Final Thought

Goals give your business purpose. They help you measure progress, stay motivated, and take real steps toward success.

Just remember:

- Pick something simple and trackable
- Break it into smaller steps
- Track your progress in a fun, clear way
- Be flexible if something needs to change
- Celebrate every step forward

You've got this. Big things happen one small goal at a time.

Chapter 9: How to Talk to Your First Customers

Before you bake 100 cupcakes, design 50 shirts, or build your own website... stop for a second.

Wouldn't it be smart to find out if people actually want what you're selling?

The best businesses don't start with guessing.

They start with **asking**.

This chapter will teach you how to talk to people — both **before** and **after** you launch — so you can learn, improve, and grow your business the smart way.

🎧 Part 1: Customer Discovery — Before You Launch
💡 What's "Customer Discovery"?

Customer discovery is a fancy term that just means **talking to people before you start** to learn what they care about, what they need, and what problems they want solved.

You don't have to be a genius or a great speaker — just curious and willing to listen.

Let's say you want to start a pet-sitting business.

You might ask neighbors:

· "What's the hardest part about having a dog when you go on

vacation?"
· "Have you ever hired a pet sitter before?"
· "What do you wish pet sitters did better?"

If you listen carefully, they'll tell you what they really need — and you can build your business around that.

Don't Ask the Wrong Questions

Here's a mistake a lot of young entrepreneurs make:

They ask, *"Do you like this idea?"* or *"Would you buy this?"*

Guess what? Most people — especially adults — will say something nice like:

"Oh yeah! That's great!"

Even if they're just being polite and would never actually buy it.

Why? Because they don't want to hurt your feelings.

Instead, ask **smart questions** that get honest answers:

· "What do you usually do when _____ happens?"
· "Have you paid for something like this before?"
· "What's been frustrating about that experience?"
· "How would you solve that problem today?"

Your job is to **learn**, not to make people say nice things.

↺ Don't Be Afraid to Pivot

Sometimes, after talking to a few people, you might realize:

· Your idea isn't solving a real problem
· There's something else they want more
· There's a better version of your idea hiding in plain sight

41

That's not failure. That's smart business.

The best entrepreneurs don't get stuck on one idea.

They **adapt** based on what they learn.

That's called a **pivot** — when you shift your plan or product to better match what people actually need.

If you're listening carefully, your future customers will point you in the right direction.

🌑 Why This Step Matters

Customer discovery saves you time, money, and frustration.

It helps you:

- Build something people actually want
- Avoid launching something nobody buys
- Start with confidence instead of guessing

Even just **five honest conversations** before you launch can make a huge difference.

📟 Part 2: Talking to Your First Real Customers — After You Launch

Once you've launched your business (even in a small way), it's time to talk to people and see how they respond.

🛆 Who Should You Talk To?

Start with people you already know:

- Friends
- Family
- Classmates
- Neighbors
- Teammates

· Teachers

These people might be your first customers — or they might give you feedback that helps you improve.

🎤 What Should You Say?

You don't need a big speech. Just be honest and friendly.
Try something like:

· "Hey, I just started a small business selling _____. Would you be open to checking it out?"
· "Can I show you something I'm working on? I'd love your opinion."
· "Would you change anything about it?"
· "Is this something you or someone you know would actually use or buy?"

You're not begging. You're learning. And the more you ask, the easier it gets.

📝 How to Ask for Feedback

Once someone tries your product or hears about your service, ask:

· What did you like?
· Was anything confusing?
· Would you use it again? Why or why not?
· Is there something that would make it even better?

Listen more than you talk.

Don't try to argue or explain too much — just take it in. Even "negative" feedback can help you grow.

If you start hearing the same comments from different people, pay attention. That's a sign!

Keep a notebook or digital note to write things down — you'll be glad you did.

🖼 What to Do with What You Learn

Once you've had a few conversations, take what you've learned and improve your business:

- Adjust your product or service
- Change your pricing
- Improve how you explain it
- Or — if needed — pivot to a new version of the idea

This is how all great businesses grow: they **talk, learn, adjust, repeat.**

What If Someone Says No?

Sometimes people say no. That's okay!

It doesn't mean your idea is bad — it might just not be right for *them*. The important thing is to:

- Stay polite
- Say thank you
- Keep going

Every "no" is just practice for the next "yes."

⊙ Final Thought

The best entrepreneurs don't try to be perfect — they try to **listen.**

So talk to people. Ask better questions. Listen for real answers.

And if you need to change your idea a little (or a lot), that's not quitting — that's growing.

Your first customers will do more than just buy from you. They'll help you build something worth sharing.

Chapter 10: How to Use AI (such as ChatGPT) as a Thought Partner

What if you had someone who could help you think, plan, write, design, and solve problems — *whenever you needed*?

Guess what? You do.

It's called AI — and it's one of the most powerful tools in the world for young entrepreneurs like you.

This chapter will show you how to use tools like **ChatGPT** to grow your business ideas, write like a pro, and get help when you're stuck. You don't need to be a tech genius — you just need curiosity and a few good questions.

💡 What Is AI (and What Can It Do)?

AI stands for **artificial intelligence**, which basically means a computer program that can "think" and "chat" with you — sort of like a robot brain that helps you with ideas, words, and plans.

It doesn't have feelings. It's not magic. It's a tool.

Think of AI like your own business sidekick. It can:

· Brainstorm ideas
· Help you write things
· Answer questions
· Explain things in a way that makes sense

46

· Even help you create simple images!

It's like having a super helpful teammate — one who never sleeps and is always ready.

What Can You Ask AI to Help With?

Here are just a few ways AI tools like ChatGPT can help you in your business:

- **Brainstorm business ideas:** "What are 5 fun business ideas for a kid who loves dogs?"
- **Create product names, slogans, or taglines:** "Help me come up with a catchy name for my lemonade stand."
- **Write product descriptions or flyers:** "Can you help me write a short ad for my slime kits?"
- **Help make checklists or plans:** "Give me a step-by-step list to start my business."
- **Fix or improve writing:** "Can you make this sound more exciting?" (and paste what you wrote)
- **Ask questions you're stuck on:** "What's the difference between profit and revenue?"
- **Get social media post ideas:** "Give me 10 funny Instagram captions for a t-shirt business."
- **Create images or logos (with help from AI image tools):** "Can you help me design a logo for my plant shop?" (Some AI tools can even turn your ideas into pictures!)

If you're ever feeling stuck — ask AI.

⊙ Ask Smart Questions, Get Better Answers

Here's the secret:

The better your question, the better the answer.

If you say, "Give me ideas," the answer will probably be boring.

If you say, "Give me 5 business ideas for a kid who likes video games and wants to help people," the answer will be way better.

Try to include:

· What kind of business you want help with
· What you like or are interested in
· What problem you're trying to solve

The more details you give, the more helpful the response will be.

👤 Remember: You're Still the Boss

AI can give you ideas — but **you make the decisions.**

If something doesn't sound right, don't use it. If it sounds cool, make it your own.

It's okay to edit, mix, or build on what AI gives you. You're the entrepreneur — AI is just your assistant.

Also: **Don't copy and paste everything** without thinking. Make sure it sounds like *you*.

👤💻 Be Smart and Stay Safe

A few quick rules to keep in mind:

· Don't share your real name, address, phone number, or email with AI tools
· If something sounds weird or doesn't make sense, ask an adult for help
· Use AI to *support* your ideas — not to *replace* your thinking
· Not everything AI says is 100% accurate — so double-check important stuff

Final Thought

AI is like a superpower for your business. It helps you move faster, think bigger, and feel more confident — especially when you're just getting started.

But the real magic isn't in the tool — it's in *you*.

AI can help you brainstorm, write, organize, and even design. But your creativity, effort, and decisions are what bring your business to life.

So next time you're stuck... ask ChatGPT a great question.

And then get back to building something amazing.

Chapter 11: Why Good Design and Branding Matter

Imagine this: You're walking through a market. Two booths are selling cookies.

The first one has cookies in plain ziplock bags. No labels. No sign.

The second one has neat packaging, a colorful logo, a small sign that says "Grandma's Famous Chocolate Chips," and it even smells amazing.

Which one would you try first?

Most people would pick the second one — even if the cookies inside are *exactly* the same.

That's the power of **design** and **branding**.

‿ What Is Branding?

Branding isn't just a logo or a color. It's the **whole experience** of your business.

Branding includes:

- Your **name**
- Your **logo**
- The **colors and fonts** you use
- Your **packaging or labels**
- The **style** of your writing (funny? serious? chill?)

- The **feeling** your business gives people
- Even the **smell**, **sound**, or **vibe** of your product or booth

Branding is like your business's personality. It's what people remember. It's how they feel when they see, hear, or even smell your product.

If you're selling handmade soap, the scent, packaging, and label all create the brand.

If you're selling t-shirts, your name, logo, and website design are part of your brand.

◉ Why Does It Matter?

Here's the truth:

People **do** judge a book by its cover.

That's why design and branding matter.

When your business **looks sharp**, people are more likely to:

- Take you seriously
- Trust that your product is good
- Remember your brand
- Tell their friends

It doesn't have to be fancy — it just has to look **clean, consistent, and intentional**.

When people see a business that looks real and professional, they believe it *is* real and professional.

◉◉ Real-Life Example

Let's say you and a friend both start lemonade stands.

- **Your stand** has a bright, clean sign, matching cups, a fun name ("Sunshine Sips"), and your prices are easy to read.

- **Your friend's stand** has a crooked cardboard sign with messy writing, no clear pricing, and random mismatched cups.

Same lemonade. Which one will get more customers?

Yours — because it looks like you care. That's branding.

🎨 You Don't Have to Be an Artist

Good design doesn't mean you need to be great at drawing or have fancy tools. You just need to keep things:

- **Simple**
- **Clear**
- **Consistent**

Here are a few easy design tips:

- Pick 1–2 colors that fit your brand (bold, soft, natural, fun)
- Pick 1–2 fonts that are easy to read
- Use the same style across your flyers, packaging, website, and social media

You can use free tools like **Canva** to help design things like:

- Logos
- Business cards
- Product labels
- Instagram posts
- Flyers or menus

🌈 Make Your Brand Feel Like *You*

Branding should match your **vibe** and your **values**.
Are you fun and energetic? Chill and natural? Sporty and bold?
Your logo, name, and colors should match that feeling.
Ask yourself:

- What feeling do I want people to get from my business?
- What do I want them to remember?

Even the name matters. "Nature Buds Plant Shop" feels different than "Leaf Legends" — even if they both sell plants. That's branding.

🔍 Small Details, Big Impact

You might think design doesn't matter much — especially when you're just starting. But people **notice** the little things:

- A sticker on your packaging
- A clean, colorful sign
- A fun logo on your website
- Matching tags or labels
- Even a great scent when they open the box

It all adds up. It tells customers:
"I care about what I'm doing — and you should too."

◉ Final Thought

Great design isn't about being fancy — it's about being clear, confident, and consistent.

When your business looks sharp, people are more likely to trust it, remember it, and support it.

So take the time to think about your brand.

Give it a name, a style, a voice — and maybe even a smell.

Because when you create something that **looks and feels real**, your customers will believe in it — and believe in *you*.

Chapter 12: How to Create the Perfect Logo

Think of your favorite brand — maybe Nike, Apple, or McDonald's.

What pops into your head first?

The logo.

The swoosh. The apple with a bite. The golden arches.

The best logos don't even need words. Just one symbol, and you instantly know the brand.

That's the power of great design.

In this chapter, you'll learn what makes a great logo, how to create one (even for free!), and why it's totally okay to start simple and improve it later.

💡 What Makes a Great Logo?

A great logo does a lot with a little. It's like the "hello" of your business — the first thing people see, and the one they'll remember.

Here are five things every great logo has:

1. **Simple** – Not too busy or detailed.
2. **Recognizable** – Easy to spot and remember.
3. **Fitting** – It matches the mood or vibe of your business.
4. **Flexible** – It looks good small, big, in color, or in black and white.
5. **Iconic** – The best logos still work even without words.

You don't need to create the next Nike swoosh — you just need something clean and clear that fits your business and feels like *you*.

What Should Your Logo Include?

There's no perfect formula, but most logos include some combination of:

- Your **business name** or initials
- A simple **symbol or icon**
- **One or two colors** that match your style
- (Optional) A short **tagline** — like "Fast. Fresh. Friendly."

Keep it simple. You want people to "get it" right away.

💰 How Much Does a Logo Cost?

Believe it or not, some big companies have paid **millions of dollars** for a single logo.

But don't worry — you don't have to.

Here are your options:

- **Free or DIY** – Use design tools and AI (see next section)
- **Affordable freelancers** – Hire someone on Fiverr.com or Upwork.com
- **Professional firms** – For more custom designs, check out TheNetMenCorp.com or Brainding.co→ *Tell them Greg L. referred you!*

No matter your budget, there's a path forward. You can always upgrade your logo later.

Tools to Help You Design One

If you want to try creating your own, here are some great tools to help:

- **Canva** – Free design tool with logo templates
- **Hatchful** by Shopify – Easy logo builder
- **Looka** or **LogoMakr** – Simple, beginner-friendly sites
- **ChatGPT (Pro version)** – Can generate logo images or brainstorm concepts
- **MidJourney** or **OpenArt.ai** – Use AI to create totally custom logo images

Just type in what you want — like "logo for a dog-walking business that's fun and modern" — and see what comes up!

🎨 Color Matters: What Are You Trying to Say?

Your logo's colors do more than just look nice — they tell people something about your business.

Here's a quick guide to **color psychology**:

- **Red** = Bold, exciting, high-energy
- **Blue** = Trustworthy, calm, smart
- **Green** = Natural, fresh, eco-friendly
- **Yellow** = Cheerful, fun, friendly
- **Black** = Strong, serious, sleek
- **Pastels** = Soft, cute, creative

Pick 1–2 colors that match your brand's vibe. Too many colors can make your logo feel messy.

👨‍💻 Make Sure It Works Everywhere

Your logo should look good on:

- Product packaging or tags
- Flyers and posters
- Your website or social media
- Stickers, business cards, or t-shirts

Test it in different sizes and backgrounds (light and dark). Can people still read it? Does it still look good small?

If yes — you're on the right track.

Don't Overthink It

Here's a secret: **most logos change over time**.

Big brands like Starbucks, Instagram, and Google have all updated or simplified their logos as they grew.

You don't need the perfect logo today. You just need one that's **good enough to start**.

So don't wait forever. Make something solid, use it, and improve it later as your business grows.

✅ Final Thought

Your logo is more than just a picture — it's the *hello* your business sends out into the world.

Whether you design it yourself using free tools, hire a freelancer, or team up with a pro firm, the most important thing is that your logo feels like **you**.

Start simple. Stay confident. And remember: you can always grow into something even better.

Chapter 13: Tips for Setting Up Your First Website

If you're mowing lawns, walking dogs, or selling friendship bracelets — do you *need* a website?

Not really.

But... it sure helps.

Having even a simple website shows people you're serious. It makes your business feel real. And it gives people a way to learn about you — even while you're sleeping.

So, whether you're starting small or dreaming big, this chapter will show you exactly how to build your first website — and make it awesome.

💡 Why Even a Simple Business Can Use a Website

Let's say you start a lawn mowing business. You get a few neighbors to hire you just by knocking on doors.

That works! But...

If you also have a simple website, you can:

- Show your prices and services
- Share customer reviews
- Post before-and-after photos of lawns
- Let people contact you at any time — even late at night

Your website is like a **24/7 flyer** that anyone can check out — even people you've never met.

You don't *have* to have one, but in today's world, it's smart to set one up.

🌐 Two Main Types of Websites

Most websites fall into two buckets:

1. **Informational**

- Explains what you do, who you are, and how to contact you
- Great for services like tutoring, dog walking, or photography

1. **E-commerce**

- Lets people buy products directly from your site
- Great for selling slime kits, stickers, t-shirts, or digital downloads

Start simple. An **informational** site is often all you need to begin.

📝 What Should Be On Your Website?

Even a basic website can make a strong impression. Here's what you should include:

- **Homepage** – A quick intro to your business
- **Products or Services Page** – What you offer, with pictures and prices
- **Contact Page** – How people can reach you (form or email)
- (Optional) **About Me Page** – Share your story as a young entrepreneur
- (Optional) **Blog or News** – If you want to share updates or tips

How to Build a Website — 3 Easy Options

You have three paths to get your website live:

1. Build It Yourself (DIY)

You can use beginner-friendly website builders like:

- **Wix**
- **Weebly**
- **Squarespace**
- **Carrd** (great for simple, one-page sites)
- **Shopify** (best for selling products online)
- **GoDaddy Website Builder**

These platforms are "drag-and-drop" — no coding needed. Many even have free plans!

2. Use AI to Help You

If you have the **paid version of ChatGPT**, you can ask it to generate a logo or website ideas. There are also AI tools like:

- **Durable.co** – builds websites instantly
- **MidJourney** or **OpenArt.ai** – can create images for your site

3. Hire a Website Designer (a.k.a. a Freelancer)

A **freelancer** is someone who works for themselves and gets hired for projects like designing websites, writing content, or creating logos.

You can find freelancers on:

- **Fiverr.com** – Many offer affordable website packages
- **Upwork.com** – Another place to find design help

If you want higher-end help, try:

- **TheNetMenCorp.com**
- **Brainding.co**→ *Be sure to tell them Greg L. sent you!*

🌐 What Is Hosting?

Once your website is built, it needs to be *hosted* somewhere so people can visit it online.

Hosting just means that your website files are stored on a computer (called a "server") that's always connected to the internet.

That way, when someone types in your website name, the page shows up!

Many website builders (like Wix or Shopify) include hosting automatically.

You can also use hosting services like:

- **GoDaddy**
- **Bluehost**
- **HostGator**

🔑 You'll Need a Domain Name

A **domain name** is your website's address — like **HappyPets.com** or **EthanDesigns.com**.

You'll need to buy one before launching your site. It usually costs about **$12–15 per year**, and you can buy it from:

- **GoDaddy.com** (recommended)
- **Namecheap.com**

🌀 How to Pick the Right Domain Name

Here are a few tips for choosing a great domain name:

- **Shorter is better**
- Good: **LilyFlowers.com**
- Not so good: **ReallyPrettyFlowersForYou.com**
- **Easy to spell and remember**
- **Avoid numbers, symbols, or hyphens**
- **Use keywords** that explain what you do
- Example: **ChicagoDogWalkers.com** is easier to find on Google

⚠ Be Careful With Trademarks

Don't use names that copy or are too close to another business's name. That could violate a **trademark** — which is a legal protection for business names, logos, or slogans.

If a name or phrase is trademarked, that means only the original business can use it. Always make sure your business name and domain name are unique and original.

Start Simple — Then Grow

Your website doesn't have to be perfect right away.

Start with one page. Add more later.

The important part is to make it **clear**, **easy to understand**, and **true to your brand**. Your website should help people know:

- Who you are
- What you offer
- How they can work with you or buy from you

✓ **Final Thought**

Your website is your **digital storefront** — it's how the world learns about you.

Whether you build it yourself or get help, the key is to **start now**. Share your story. Show what you do. Be proud of it.

Once it's live, send people the link and let them know:

"This is my business. I made it. And I'm open for business."

Chapter 14: What Is a Trademark — and Why Should You Care?

Let's say you start a business selling awesome stickers. You name it **"Arizona Stickers"**, make a logo, and start selling to friends and neighbors.

Things are going great — until one day, you get an email that says:

"Sorry, but there's already a company called *Arizona Sticker Company*, and they've trademarked that name. You can't use it."

Uh oh.

Now you have to change your name, your logo, maybe your website. Total bummer.

That's why this chapter exists.

It's time to learn about **trademarks** — and how to protect your business before problems show up.

💡 What's a Trademark?

A **trademark** is a legal way to protect:

- Your **business name**
- Your **logo or symbol**
- Your **slogan or phrase**

When you register a trademark, it means no one else is allowed to use that same name or logo in your line of work. And if *you* use someone else's trademark — even by accident — you might be asked to stop, or even face legal trouble.

🏠 Real-Life Examples

- Only **Nike** can use the word "Nike" and their famous swoosh on sneakers
- Only **LEGO** can use their name and block design for toys
- Only **Coca-Cola** can use that exact name and logo for soda

That's how businesses protect what makes them unique.

☺ Why Should You Care as a Kid?

Even if you're just starting out, it's a smart move to:

- Make sure your business name and logo are **original**
- Avoid using something that already belongs to someone else
- Be ready to protect your brand if it grows big

You're building something real — and real businesses take care of their names.

❤ Pick a Name That's Truly Yours

Here's a rule to remember:

"If it sounds or looks too much like another business name, it's probably not a good idea."

So if there's already a business called **"Arizona Sticker Company,"** don't name yours **"Arizona Stickers."** That's confusing, and it might even be considered trademark infringement.

Choose a name that is:

- Unique
- Easy to remember
- Easy to spell
- Not too close to another business

🔍 How to Search for Trademarks

You can do a free trademark search at **USPTO.gov**:

1. Click on **"Search Trademarks"**
2. Type in your business name idea
3. See what pops up

If you see a name that's very close to yours — especially in your same type of business — you might want to pick something else.

👁 Heads up: There's a little art to this. Professionals who do trademark searches can spot conflicts even if the names are spelled differently but sound the same.

How to Register Your Own Trademark

If your business starts growing and you want to protect your name and logo, you can **register your own trademark** in the U.S.

Here's how:

- ✅ **Do it yourself** at USPTO.gov
- ✅ Use a service like:
- LegalZoom.com
- TrademarkEngine.com
- RocketLawyer.com
- ✅ Or hire a **trademark lawyer** who knows the process

🎟 Cost: Usually around **$250–350 or more**, depending on how you file. That's why most kid-run businesses wait until they're growing before registering.

But no matter what — even *before* you register, you should make sure your name is original.

✐ What You Can (and Can't) Trademark
✅ You CAN trademark:

- Unique business names (like "ChocoBeast Energy Bars")
- Logos (like a special badge or icon)
- Slogans (like "Powered by Chocolate")

✕ You CAN'T trademark:

- Common words like "Books" or "T-Shirts"
- Names that are already taken
- Anything that's too close to an existing brand

✅ Final Thought

"Your brand is your identity — don't build it on someone else's foundation."

You don't need to file a trademark right away, especially if your business is just starting.

But you *do* need to make sure your name, logo, or slogan doesn't belong to someone else.

Be original. Be smart. And protect the thing you're building — because it just might grow into something big.

Chapter 15: What Type of Entity Should I Set Up?

(Bonus Chapter – Only if You're Ready!)

Let's say you're running a business that's starting to take off. Maybe you're making real money. Maybe you're even selling products to people you've never met.

Someone asks, "Are you an LLC or a sole proprietorship?"

And you're like... "Uhhh... what?"

Don't worry! This chapter is here to help.

⚲ Do I *Need* to Set Something Up?

If you're:

- Mowing lawns
- Selling slime
- Tutoring your neighbors

Then no — you probably don't need to register anything yet.

Most kids start out running a business as a **sole proprietorship** — which just means *you are the business*. There's nothing to register. You can just go for it.

But as you grow, or if your business gets more complex, you might need to "make it official." That's where **business entities** come in.

What's a Business Entity, Anyway?

A **business entity** is just the *official setup* of your business. It helps answer:

- Who owns the business?
- How are taxes handled?
- Who is legally responsible if something goes wrong?

There are different types of entities — some are super simple, and others are made for big companies with lots of employees.

⚠ What Is Liability (And Why It Matters)

Here's a word you'll hear a lot: **liability.**

Liability is about **who's responsible** if something bad happens in your business — like:

- Someone gets hurt using your product
- A customer complains or sues
- You owe money for a mistake

If you're a sole proprietor, **you** are personally responsible. That means your savings, allowance money, even your bike could be at risk.

That's why some businesses eventually create an **LLC**, which helps separate the business from the person.

✓ Option 1: Sole Proprietorship (Most Kids Start Here)

This is the **most common setup for young entrepreneurs**.

- You don't need to fill out forms
- You can use your own name or a business name (called a "DBA" or *Doing Business As*)

· You keep all the profits
· But: You also take all the risk

When your business is small and simple, a sole proprietorship is a great way to start. As long as you're not doing anything risky, it usually works just fine.

Option 2: LLC (Limited Liability Company)
An **LLC** is a step up in professionalism — and protection.

· It creates a wall between your personal stuff and your business
· If something goes wrong, only the business is affected — not you personally
· It's great if you're earning real money or selling online

Forming an LLC costs money and requires paperwork. But if your business is growing, it might be worth it (with adult help, of course).

🕹 Option 3: Corporation (Inc.)
This is how big companies like Apple or Nike are set up.

· It's complex, with lots of rules and paperwork
· It's good for raising money or having lots of investors
· You probably don't need this unless you're building the next Amazon

It's good to know it exists — just not something most young entrepreneurs need to worry about.

🌐 How to Set Up an Entity (If You Want To)
If you decide it's time to form something official, you'll need an

adult to help. You can:

- Register through your **state's official government website**
- Or use easy online services like:
- LegalZoom.com
- Incfile.com
- BizFilings.com

These companies help with the paperwork and guide you through the process.

It usually costs **between $50 and $300**, depending on where you live and what type of entity you choose.

👦📋 Ask a Grown-Up When You're Ready

You don't have to figure all of this out by yourself.

If your business is starting to:

- Make real money
- Sell to people outside your family or school
- Handle customer data or risky products
- Or if you're opening a business bank account

Then it's time to have a conversation with a parent, guardian, or expert about next steps.

✅ Final Thought

"Start simple, grow smart."

You don't have to set up a fancy business structure on Day One.

But as you get bigger, it's helpful to understand your options — and protect the awesome thing you're building.

Just like a house needs a good foundation, your business will eventually need one too.

So now you know. And when you're ready, you'll be one step ahead.

Chapter 16: How to Keep Track of Your Expenses

You sold lemonade and made $100. Awesome, right?

But wait... you spent $10 on lemons, $5 on sugar, $3 on cups, and $2 on poster board for your signs. That's $20 spent.

So your real profit wasn't $100 — it was **$80**.

That's why smart entrepreneurs always **track their money**. It's one of the most important things you can do in your business — no matter how big or small it is.

Let's break it down.

💰 Income vs. Expenses

You've probably heard these words before, but here's what they mean in business:

- **Income** = the money you **earn** (from selling products, doing chores, walking dogs, etc.)
- **Expenses** = the money you **spend** (on supplies, shipping, ads, tools, etc.)

Your **profit** is what's left after you subtract expenses from income:

Income – Expenses = Profit

If you don't know your expenses, you might *think* you're making money... when you're really not.

✍ Start Simple: Just Write It Down

At the beginning, you don't need fancy software. A notebook works just fine.

You can make two columns:

- Column 1: **Money In** (every time someone pays you)
- Column 2: **Money Out** (every time you buy something for your business)

Date	Money In	What Was It?	Money Out	What Was It?
April 5	$10	Sold 2 dog walks	$0	–
April 6	$20	Sold slime kits	$5	Bought glue
April 7	$0	–	$2	Printed flyers

Kid-Friendly Tracking Apps

There are also apps built for kids that help you track money:

- **BusyKid** – lets you track chores, earnings, and spending
- **Greenlight** – helps manage money and even lets you set up savings goals

Just ask a parent before downloading anything.

◉ Want to Be More Professional? Meet QuickBooks

As your business grows, you might want to use what most adult businesses use: **QuickBooks**.

QuickBooks is software that tracks:

- All your income and expenses
- Invoices (money people owe you)
- Inventory and supplies
- Taxes

You'll definitely need help from an **adult** to set it up — and possibly someone called a **bookkeeper** or an **accountant**.

What's a Bookkeeper or an Accountant?

Let's break it down:

- A **bookkeeper** is someone who helps organize all your money records — like keeping track of what comes in and what goes out
- An **accountant** helps with **taxes** and gives financial advice, especially when your business starts making real money

You probably don't need either right now, but it's helpful to know that as your business gets bigger, you can ask for help with the money side of things.

▥ The Three Numbers You Must Track

Even if your business is small, try to always track:

1. **What you earned** (total money in)
2. **What you spent** (total money out)
3. **What's left over** (your profit)

That's it! Just those three things will help you make smart decisions.

🔍 Bonus Tip: Track Other Stuff Too

A smart business owner doesn't just track money — they track **activity**.

"If you don't measure it, you can't manage it."

You can track:

- How many flyers you hand out each week
- How many people visited your website
- How many jars of cookies or bottles of fertilizer you sold
- How many customers came back and bought again

Little numbers help you see big patterns. And big patterns help you grow.

✅ Final Thought

"Businesses that stay organized don't guess — they *know*."

You don't need to be a math wizard. You just need to **write stuff down**.

Start with a notebook or a spreadsheet. Later, you can use apps or even hire help. Just remember: if you stay on top of your numbers, your business will always be stronger, smarter, and ready to grow.

Chapter 17: How to Source Products and Find Suppliers

Let's say you come up with an amazing idea — a glow-in-the-dark pencil case with your own custom logo. You've sketched it out, picked your colors, and even named your brand.

There's just one problem...

You don't know how to sew. You don't own a factory. You're not even sure how to get it made.

That's okay! Most entrepreneurs don't make their products themselves. Instead, they use something called **sourcing** — and in this chapter, you'll learn how it works.

🔍 What Is Sourcing?

Sourcing means finding someone to help you make or supply your product. It could be:

- A person in your community (like a local artist or sewing shop)
- A business that already sells something similar
- A large factory — sometimes even in another country

Sourcing is how businesses turn ideas into real products. You come up with the vision, and someone else helps you bring it to life.

🌎 Where Can You Find Suppliers?

Here are a few options:

1. Make it yourself

You or a family member might be able to create the first batch of products at home.

2. Find local help

Maybe a local print shop, artist, or craftsperson can help you make things.

3. Work with a factory

This is what bigger businesses do — and what many kid entrepreneurs eventually try too!

🌐 Helpful Websites for Sourcing

These websites connect you with manufacturers or suppliers:

- **Alibaba.com** – A massive platform with factories around the world (mostly in China)
- **Faire.com** – U.S. and international suppliers who sell in smaller batches
- **MakersRow.com** – A great way to find U.S.-based factories

Always explore these sites with the help of a **parent or trusted adult**.

🗺 What to Know About Alibaba

Alibaba is one of the most popular websites for finding factories. It's a great place to search for:

- Custom products
- Packaging and labels
- Gadgets, clothing, and more

But be careful:

- You might be talking to an **agent**, not the actual factory. Agents are middlemen — they know factories but aren't making the product themselves. This isn't always bad, but ideally, you want to talk **directly to the factory**.

Also, if you use **Alibaba's Trade Assurance**, they can help protect your order if something goes wrong.

💬 What to Ask Suppliers

When you contact a supplier (always with adult help), here are smart questions to ask:

- Can I see a **sample** first?
- What is your **Minimum Order Quantity** (MOQ)?
- How much does each item cost?
- What are the **shipping costs**?
- How long will it take to make and deliver?

🛖 Go to a Tradeshow!

Want to learn even faster? Visit a **tradeshow** with your parent or guardian!

A tradeshow is like a giant convention where factories set up booths and show off their products. You can:

- See samples in person
- Ask questions face-to-face
- Compare different factories quickly

If you're interested in clothing or fashion, check out the **MAGIC Apparel Show** in Las Vegas — it has a special "Sourcing" section where you can meet real manufacturers.

Even just walking around a tradeshow is a powerful learning experience.

🏵 Watch Out for Payment Scams

"Never wire full payment to someone you don't know."

Unfortunately, some people online pretend to be factories — then disappear with your money. That's why it's super important to:

- Use **safe payment methods** like:
- **Alibaba Trade Assurance**
- **PayPal**
- **Escrow services** (they hold your money until the product arrives)
- Never send large amounts upfront — especially not through direct bank transfers or Western Union
- Let an **adult handle payments** and double-check everything

If something sounds too good to be true... it probably is.

🎁 Understand the *Real* Cost of a Product

When you're calculating how much your product costs, remember:

✔ **Factory price** – What the supplier charges per item

+ Shipping cost – Can be very expensive if it's coming from Asia or far away

+ Tariffs or import taxes – Extra government fees when products enter your country

These added costs can really change the price of your product — so always ask for the total cost delivered to your door!

💡 **Smart Sourcing Tips**

- Always start **small** — ask for 1 or 2 samples first
- Never feel bad asking questions — this is how you learn
- Talk to **lots of factories** to compare prices and get educated
- Take notes, save emails, and stay organized
- Don't rush — sourcing is a process, not a race
- Work with a **parent or adult** at every step

✔ **Final Thought**

"Great entrepreneurs don't do it all themselves — they find the right people to help."

Sourcing lets you turn your idea into a real product — even if you can't make it yourself. It takes time, questions, and patience. But it's also exciting. You're building real business muscles!

So don't be afraid to start the conversation. Ask a factory how something is made. Get a sample. Learn. That's how it all begins.

Chapter 18: Work On Your Business, Not Just In It

Imagine this:

You're running a slime business. You make the slime. You package it. You write the thank-you notes. You tape up the boxes. You take them to the post office. You do *everything*.

That's called **working in your business** — and it's how most entrepreneurs start.

But what if you wanted to grow? Or take a break? Or let your little brother help?

You'd need a system. And that's when you start **working on your business** — not just in it.

This idea comes from a book called **The E-Myth Revisited: Why Most Small Businesses Don't Work And What To Do About It** by Michael Gerber. It's a book for adults, but the lesson is simple:

The most successful businesses aren't built by people who do everything. They're built by people who create systems that help everything run smoothly — even when they're not there.

⚲ What's the Difference?

Here's what it looks like:

Working *in* your business

- You're the one doing all the work
- You pack every order
- You make every delivery
- You answer every message

Working *on* your business

- You create a system for packing so someone else can help
- You build a calendar for deliveries
- You make a script for responding to customers

One makes you busy. The other makes you powerful.

✓ What Is a System?

A **system** is just a simple, repeatable way of doing something.

It's a checklist.

A guide.

A plan.

If you had to teach someone else how to do something in your business, could they follow your steps?

If the answer is yes — you've got a system!

💡 Real Example: Packing Slime Orders

Let's go back to your slime business.

You decide to draw a step-by-step guide for how to pack your slime kits. It looks something like this:

1. Put the label on the jar
2. Check that the lid is tight
3. Place slime into the box
4. Add a thank-you card

5. Seal the box with tape
6. Attach the shipping label

Now your little brother or sister could follow your guide and help you pack orders — without making a mess or asking a hundred questions.

You're not just making slime.

You're building a system.

And that's what real entrepreneurs do.

✎ Easy Systems You Can Build (Right Now)

Here are just a few ideas for systems you can create in your own business:

- A checklist for what to bring to your lemonade stand
- A step-by-step guide for cleaning up after pet-sitting
- A daily schedule for checking and replying to messages
- A script for introducing yourself to a potential customer
- A list of supplies to reorder each week

Systems don't have to be fancy. They just have to be clear.

Tools You Can Use to Build Systems

You can create systems using:

- A **notebook** or checklist
- **Google Docs or Sheets**
- A drawing or diagram
- A printed sign you hang near your workspace
- A short **video** or voice memo if writing isn't your favorite

Some people even make little "how-to" binders for their business.

Start small. Start simple.

Why Systems Matter So Much

When you build systems:

- You can **ask others for help**
- You **make fewer mistakes**
- You **save time**
- You can **grow your business**
- And yes... you might even get a day off!

Even giant companies like McDonald's or Amazon rely on systems. That's why your McDonald's order is pretty much the same whether you're in New York, Texas, or California — they've built systems that anyone can follow.

Start Thinking Like a Boss

Here's the secret:

You don't have to wait until you have employees.

You don't need to be "big" to start building like a pro.

If you can write down how something should be done — you're already building your business like a real entrepreneur.

Final Thought

"If you want to grow, step back and start building."

You don't have to do everything forever. You can create systems that let your friends, siblings, or even hired helpers do some of the work.

Start by writing one small checklist.

Then another.

Before long, you're not just running a business — you're building one that can run *without* you doing every single thing.

And that's the difference between being busy... and being brilliant.

Chapter 19: How to Handle Failure and Bounce Back

Have you ever tried something that didn't work out the way you hoped? I encourage you to never consider this failure. With the right mindset, there really is no such thing as failure – only experiments that help you find what really works. In business, not everything goes perfectly the first time. Sometimes your idea needs a tweak, a new approach, or a total pivot. That doesn't mean you've failed – it just means you're getting closer to the right answer. In this chapter, you'll learn how to see every setback as part of the process, how to adjust and improve your ideas, and how to keep moving forward with confidence. Because the truth is, every successful entrepreneur knows that what doesn't work is just as important as what does.

1. The First Try Doesn't Always Work — And That's Okay

"You're not building a perfect business. You're building a strong one."

- Every entrepreneur faces setbacks
- Failure isn't the end — it's just feedback
- The best business owners use failure as fuel to improve

2. Real-World Examples of Failure Before Success

- Walt Disney, Michael Jordan, and other icons
- Most great businesses start with rough drafts and wrong turns

3. What "Failure" Might Look Like in a Kid Business

- No one shows up to your booth
- You spend money and make no sales
- Your idea works at first... then fizzles
- People give critical feedback

All of this is normal — and useful. And again, I wouldn't consider any of this failure.

4. Embrace Hiccups — Don't Fear Them
"The strongest people aren't scared of failure. They accept it, learn from it, and grow."

- Failure helps you grow faster
- Powerful entrepreneurs embrace the process, even the messy parts
- Failure = valuable information

5. You Only Fail If You Quit

- If you keep going, adjusting, and improving — you haven't failed
- Real failure only happens when you give up completely and stop learning

6. Know When to Pivot or Stop (and Why That's Not Quitting)

"Sometimes the smartest move is to stop and shift direction."

- Stopping doesn't always mean failure — it means you're thinking clearly
- Some businesses or ideas aren't meant to last forever
- Changing your approach is a **strategy**, not a loss
- Learning when to pivot is a sign of maturity and wisdom

7. What to Do When Things Go Wrong

1. Take a breath
2. Look at what happened
3. Ask what you can learn
4. Talk to someone you trust
5. Adjust or pivot
6. Try again — in a smarter way

8. Use Feedback and Evolve

- Great businesses listen and adjust
- Build a feedback loop into your process
- Write down lessons from mistakes
- Stay flexible and open to improvement

9. What Worked Yesterday Might Not Work Tomorrow

"Great businesses evolve with the world."

- Be ready to refresh or reinvent your idea
- Stay curious, stay honest, and don't get stuck

10. Final Thought

"You didn't fail — you changed directions. That's called growth."

Every time something goes wrong, you get better.

Every decision to pivot makes you stronger.

The best entrepreneurs don't just bounce back — they bounce forward.

And remember, there is no such thing as failure. Keep learning, keep adjusting, push forward.

II

Ideas List

This part is all about inspiration. You'll find 108 different business ideas that kids like you can start. Some are super simple. Others are more creative or unique. Each idea gives you a short overview, explains why it might work, who your customers could be, steps to get started, and tips to make it even better. You don't have to do them all—just find one that fits you, start small, and learn as you go!

Ideas List

Before You Dive In...

There are lots of different kinds of businesses in this book—some where you sell a product (like a bookmark or T-shirt), some where you offer a service (like mowing lawns or walking dogs), and some you run totally online (like designing digital downloads).

We didn't label each idea by category on purpose. Instead, just read through them and see what gets you excited! Some might be physical, some digital, some both. The goal is to spark ideas and help you get started—your way.

Idea 1: Custom Bookmark Business

1. What's the Idea?

Make and sell colorful, handmade bookmarks using cardstock, markers, stickers, and ribbon. These are fun to create and easy to sell to classmates, teachers, or at school book fairs and events.

2. Why It Could Work

Bookmarks are low-cost to make but highly personal and useful. Kids and adults alike enjoy buying small, creative items—especially when they're themed or handmade. This is a great way to combine art and entrepreneurship.

3. Who Might Be Your Customer?

- Friends and classmates who enjoy reading
- Teachers and school librarians
- Parents looking for small gifts or stocking stuffers
- Book fair visitors or craft market shoppers

4. Steps to Get Started (and Budget)

Estimated Startup Budget: Under $20

- Buy cardstock or sturdy paper (you may already have some at home)
- Use markers, pens, and stickers to design 10–15 bookmarks
- Ask a few people for feedback on your designs
- Price them at $1–$2 each (offer bundle deals for 3–5 bookmarks)
- Sell at school events, gift tables, or to family friends
- Optional: add ribbon or laminate for a more professional look

5. Pro Tips

- Make themed collections (holidays, animals, favorite book series, school spirit)
- Keep your designs neat and bold—thin lines may not show up well when printed
- Consider using Canva or another free design app if you want to explore digital versions for future sales

Tags: Creative, School-Friendly, Low Budget, Easy to Start

Good for kids who: Love art, reading, or making small, personalized gifts

Idea 2: Slime Kit Business

1. What's the Idea?

Create and sell fun DIY slime kits that include ingredients and step-by-step instructions. These are perfect for classmates, parties, or craft fairs.

2. Why It Could Work

Slime is always in style with kids! A kit makes it easy and mess-free for others to make their own slime at home without gathering the supplies.

3. Who Might Be Your Customer?

- Friends and classmates
- Parents buying party favors or gifts
- Craft fair shoppers

4. Steps to Get Started (and Budget)

Estimated Startup Budget: $20–$50

- Learn a basic slime recipe and test a few batches
- Buy ingredients in bulk: glue, baking soda, contact solution, glitter, mix-ins
- Package each kit in ziplock bags or plastic containers with clear labels and instructions
- Set a price ($5–$10 per kit)
- Sell at school events, local fairs, or with parent help online

5. Pro Tips

- Offer scent and color choices (e.g., peppermint glitter slime!)
- Create holiday or seasonal slime collections
- Make a "build your own kit" menu for customization

Tags: Creative, School-Friendly, Moderate Budget

Good for kids who: Love crafts, science experiments, and getting hands-on

Idea 3: Friendship Bracelets

1. What's the Idea?

Make and sell colorful friendship bracelets using embroidery thread and beads. Sell individually or in themed bundles.

2. Why It Could Work

Bracelets are fun, easy to make, and great for gifting. Personalized or custom-color styles can boost popularity.

3. Who Might Be Your Customer?

- Classmates and friends
- Campers or teammates
- People looking for small, affordable gifts

4. Steps to Get Started (and Budget)

Estimated Startup Budget: Under $20

- Learn simple knotting or braiding techniques
- Buy colorful embroidery floss, string, or beads

- Create a collection of samples
- Price at $1–$3 each (offer bundles too!)
- Sell at school, sports events, or local fairs

5. Pro Tips

- Offer custom-name or initial bracelets
- Use school colors or holiday themes
- Create a "BFF Pack" with matching sets

Tags: Creative, Fashion-Friendly, Low Budget

Good for kids who: Enjoy jewelry-making, crafts, and trends

Idea 4: Painted Rock Shop

1. What's the Idea?

Collect smooth rocks, paint them with cool designs or inspiring messages, and sell them as decorations, paperweights, or gifts.

2. Why It Could Work

Painted rocks are fun to make and easy to personalize. People love buying small, handmade items that spread positivity.

3. Who Might Be Your Customer?

- Teachers
- Parents or relatives
- Craft fair shoppers

4. Steps to Get Started (and Budget)

Estimated Startup Budget: Under $20

- Collect smooth rocks (from outdoors or buy in bulk)
- Paint designs with acrylics — emojis, animals, quotes

- Optional: spray seal them for protection
- Set pricing from $1–$5 based on size and detail
- Sell individually or in themed gift sets

5. Pro Tips

- Create "kindness rocks" with uplifting messages
- Offer custom-painted names or pet portraits
- Package with tags or mini gift bags

Tags: Creative, Nature-Inspired, Low Budget

Good for kids who: Like art, outdoor activities, and spreading kindness

Idea 5: Custom Stickers or Labels

1. What's the Idea?

Design and sell custom stickers with fun graphics, quotes, or drawings. You can print them yourself or use a print service.

2. Why It Could Work

Stickers are super popular and easy to produce. They work great for laptops, notebooks, water bottles, and more.

3. Who Might Be Your Customer?

- Students
- Teachers (for rewards)
- Kids who love decorating their stuff

4. Steps to Get Started (and Budget)

Estimated Startup Budget: $20–$50

- Design your stickers with Canva, Procreate, or by hand
- Print at home on sticker paper or order from a site like Sticker

Mule
- Package in bundles (3–5 per set)
- Set prices at $3–$6 per pack
- Sell at school or with help from a parent online

5. Pro Tips

- Create themed collections (pets, school jokes, books)
- Offer waterproof or holographic upgrades
- Test what designs get the most attention before printing in bulk

Tags: Digital Design, Creative, Moderate Budget

Good for kids who: Like graphic design, clever ideas, or customizing school gear

Idea 6: DIY Bath Bomb Kits

1. What's the Idea?

Make and sell fizzy, scented bath bomb kits with colorful ingredients and simple instructions. These make great gifts and are fun for kids and adults alike.

2. Why It Could Work

Bath bombs are popular, especially for birthdays and holiday gifts. Selling the kits (instead of finished bombs) lets people enjoy making them at home—and keeps your costs lower.

3. Who Might Be Your Customer?

- Parents shopping for gift ideas
- Kids who enjoy self-care or spa activities
- Craft fair and holiday market shoppers

4. Steps to Get Started (and Budget)

Estimated Startup Budget: $20–$50

- Buy ingredients like baking soda, citric acid, cornstarch, essential oils, and colorants
- Practice a few recipes first
- Package dry ingredients into kits with printed instructions
- Add cute packaging or themed labels
- Price each kit around $5–$10 and sell as singles or bundles

5. Pro Tips

- Make themed kits (spa night, birthday gift, holiday colors)
- Offer different scents (lavender, peppermint, citrus)
- Add extras like a ribbon, mini spoon, or bath bomb mold

Tags: Creative, Self-Care, Moderate Budget

Good for kids who: Enjoy mixing, gifting, and making things smell amazing

Idea 7: DIY Dog Treats

1. What's the Idea?

Bake your own dog treats using safe ingredients and sell them to local pet owners or at community events.

2. Why It Could Work

People love spoiling their pets with homemade treats! Many owners prefer natural snacks over store-bought brands.

3. Who Might Be Your Customer?

- Dog owners in your neighborhood
- Family friends and relatives with pets
- People attending dog parks or pet fairs

4. Steps to Get Started (and Budget)

Estimated Startup Budget: Under $20

- With adult help, test simple recipes using dog-safe ingredients like oats, peanut butter, and pumpkin

- Bake, cool, and package treats with clear ingredient labels
- Set your price ($3–$5 per bag)
- Offer free samples and encourage feedback
- Sell locally or at pet events (with adult supervision)

5. Pro Tips

- Use bone- or paw-shaped cookie cutters
- Make birthday treat packs with a fun label
- Offer custom name tags for the treat bags

Tags: Animal-Friendly, School-Friendly, Low Budget

Good for kids who: Love dogs, baking, and helping pet parents

Idea 8: Yard Work Help

1. What's the Idea?

Offer to help neighbors with basic yard work like pulling weeds, raking leaves, or watering plants.

2. Why It Could Work

Not everyone has time—or energy—for yard chores. A helpful kid offering a fair price is often appreciated by busy adults or older neighbors.

3. Who Might Be Your Customer?

- Neighbors with gardens or lawns
- Family friends
- Elderly residents or busy parents

4. Steps to Get Started (and Budget)

Estimated Startup Budget: Under $50

- Borrow or use basic tools like gloves, rake, or watering can

- Make a list of services and simple pricing
- Ask neighbors or family if they need help
- Track your clients and keep a schedule
- Be consistent and polite to earn repeat business

5. Pro Tips

- Offer seasonal bundles (e.g., "Spring Clean-Up Package")
- Wear bright, clean clothes and show up on time
- Ask for reviews or referrals to grow faster

Tags: Active, Outdoors, Service-Based

Good for kids who: Like working outside and staying physically active

Idea 9: Water Bottle Refill Station

1. What's the Idea?

Set up a mobile water refill station at sports practices or local events and offer water for a small fee or tips.

2. Why It Could Work

People get thirsty at games and outdoor events! A refill station is useful, low-cost, and environmentally friendly.

3. Who Might Be Your Customer?

- Athletes at school or local practices
- Parents, coaches, and event attendees
- Park-goers or concert crowds

4. Steps to Get Started (and Budget)

Estimated Startup Budget: Under $50

- Use a large water jug or cooler and set up a table
- Bring cups, funnels, or reusable bottle options

- Create a fun sign and donation jar
- Offer refills for $0.25 or tips
- Keep it clean, friendly, and cheerful

5. Pro Tips

- Bring music or wear a "Water Hero" badge
- Offer ice water on hot days
- Use compostable cups or promote reusable bottles

Tags: Event-Friendly, Outdoors, Eco-Conscious

Good for kids who: Are social, energetic, and enjoy helping at games or events

Idea 10: Mini Comic Book Creator

1. What's the Idea?

Write and illustrate short comic books, then print, fold, and staple them into mini-books to sell or trade.

2. Why It Could Work

Comics are fun, collectible, and creative. A personalized mini-comic can be a unique gift or school-friendly product.

3. Who Might Be Your Customer?

- Classmates or siblings
- Comic fans and collectors
- Parents and teachers looking for fun reading gifts

4. Steps to Get Started (and Budget)

Estimated Startup Budget: Under $20

- Come up with characters and a short story
- Draw 5–10 comic pages and scan or photocopy them

- Use AI to help powerful interesting images
- Print, fold, and staple into mini-booklets
- Price each one at $2–$5 or offer bundles
- Sell at book fairs, school events, or online (with parent help)

5. Pro Tips

- Offer personalization (e.g., draw your customer as a superhero!)
- Make themed editions (sports, fantasy, funny animals)
- Collaborate with a friend who writes or draws

Tags: Creative, Book Lover, Low Budget

Good for kids who: Love storytelling, drawing, and making people laugh

Idea 11: Upcycled Art Projects

1. What's the Idea?

Turn recyclable items like bottle caps, cardboard, or magazines into cool art pieces or decorations, then sell them at school events or art fairs.

2. Why It Could Work

People love eco-friendly and creative gifts. Turning "trash into treasure" is fun, unique, and great for the planet.

3. Who Might Be Your Customer?

- Teachers and librarians
- Parents shopping for gifts
- Craft fair shoppers and art fans

4. Steps to Get Started (and Budget)

Estimated Startup Budget: Under $20

- Gather clean recyclable materials from home or neighbors

- Use glue, tape, and paints to create wall art, signs, or decor
- Set up a small display or "mini gallery" at school or local events
- Price items based on size and time it took to make
- Offer before-and-after photos to show how each item was transformed

5. Pro Tips

- Make themed sets (e.g., "Ocean Trash Art" or "Magazine Mosaic Signs")
- Write a short story or description for each piece
- Keep your work neat, safe, and well-labeled

Tags: Creative, Eco-Friendly, Low Budget

Good for kids who: Love art, recycling, and thinking outside the box

Idea 12: Button & Pin Creation

1. What's the Idea?

Design and make custom buttons or pins with fun sayings, school spirit themes, or original artwork.

2. Why It Could Work

Pins are trendy, easy to collect, and fun to wear on backpacks, jackets, or pencil cases. Great for clubs, events, or gift packs.

3. Who Might Be Your Customer?

- Students at your school
- Teachers for class prizes
- Club members or sports teams

4. Steps to Get Started (and Budget)

Estimated Startup Budget: $20–$50

- Use a button-making machine or kit (available online)
- Design artwork by hand or digitally

- Print and assemble into 1–2 inch buttons
- Display on a pin board or cardboard stand
- Price at $1–$3 each or sell bundles for $5+

5. Pro Tips

- Create a "pin-of-the-month" series
- Offer custom designs for birthdays or clubs
- Try school-themed collections and mascot pins

Tags: School-Friendly, Creative, Moderate Budget

Good for kids who: Like graphic design, wearable art, and pop culture trends

Idea 13: Mini Succulent Planters

1. What's the Idea?

Decorate small pots and plant mini succulents to sell as gifts, desk decor, or study buddies.

2. Why It Could Work

Succulents are super cute, easy to care for, and popular with kids and adults. These mini planters make perfect thank-you gifts or classroom decorations.

3. Who Might Be Your Customer?

- Teachers and school staff
- Parents and neighbors
- Students wanting a mini desk plant

4. Steps to Get Started (and Budget)

Estimated Startup Budget: $20–$50

- Buy or reuse small pots (ceramic, plastic, or recycled containers)

- Decorate the pots with paint, stickers, or markers
- Add soil and succulents (or create DIY kits with care cards)
- Price each plant around $4–$10 depending on size
- Sell at school, markets, or online (with parent help)

5. Pro Tips

- Name your plants (e.g., "Spike," "Sunny," "Captain Cactus")
- Market as "Stress Busters" or "Study Buddies"
- Offer discounts for teacher appreciation week or holidays

Tags: Creative, Nature-Inspired, Moderate Budget

Good for kids who: Like decorating, nature, and giving thoughtful gifts

Idea 14: Recycled Crayon Shapes

1. What's the Idea?

Melt down old or broken crayons into fun new shapes (stars, animals, hearts) and sell them as cool art supplies or party favors.

2. Why It Could Work

It's colorful, useful, and eco-friendly. Kids love getting fun-shaped crayons, and parents like the idea of reusing instead of throwing away.

3. Who Might Be Your Customer?

- Parents and teachers
- Party planners or classmates
- Kids who like art supplies with personality

4. Steps to Get Started (and Budget)

Estimated Startup Budget: Under $20

- Collect old crayons from friends, family, or classrooms
- Break into small pieces and melt in silicone molds **(only with adult

help)
- Let cool and pop them out
- Package into bundles with labels
- Sell for $2–$5 per set depending on size

5. Pro Tips

- Offer holiday shapes (e.g., pumpkins, hearts, snowflakes)
- Create rainbow swirl crayons by mixing colors
- Make custom party packs with names

Tags: Creative, Eco-Friendly, Low Budget

Good for kids who: Love crafts, recycling, and colorful creations

Idea 15: LEGO Mini-Pack Resale

1. What's the Idea?

Sort and repackage used LEGO pieces into fun, themed mini-packs for resale, trading, or gift sets.

2. Why It Could Work

LEGO fans are always looking for cool new parts or themes. Mini-packs feel like surprises and can be resold easily at events or online.

3. Who Might Be Your Customer?

- Other LEGO-loving kids
- Parents buying gifts or stocking stuffers
- Toy collectors or party planners

4. Steps to Get Started (and Budget)

Estimated Startup Budget: $20–$50

- Gather used LEGOs (from your own sets or donated extras)
- Clean and sort by color or theme

- Package into small kits with 20–50 pieces
- Create cool labels like "Space Pack" or "Mini Vehicles"
- Sell at events or online with help from an adult

5. Pro Tips

- Offer mystery bags for extra fun
- Build and photograph sample creations to inspire buyers
- Include a mini instruction card or challenge ("Build a robot!")

Tags: Creative, Toy-Based, Moderate Budget

Good for kids who: Love LEGOs, organizing, and sharing creativity

Idea 16: Custom Puzzle Creator

1. What's the Idea?

Design your own puzzles using original artwork, funny themes, or even customer-submitted photos. You can make them by hand or use print-on-demand services to create fun, personalized gifts and games.

2. Why It Could Work

Puzzles are a great screen-free activity for families, classrooms, and parties. People love personalized gifts, and unique puzzles make perfect birthday, holiday, or rainy-day surprises.

3. Who Might Be Your Customer?

Parents buying gifts

Teachers for classroom activities

Kids looking for fun, creative games

Friends and family who love something handmade

4. Steps to Get Started (and Budget)

Estimated Startup Budget: $10–$50

Draw or design original artwork or create fun themes

Option 1: Print on paper or cardboard and hand-cut with templates

Option 2: Use a site like Printify or Shutterfly to order custom puzzles from your design or photos

Package in small boxes or envelopes with a preview image

Set your prices ($5–$15 depending on size or customization level)

Sell at school events, online (with a parent), or by word of mouth

5. Pro Tips

Offer themes like pets, holidays, silly animals, or classroom jokes

Allow buyers to send in their own photos to turn into puzzles

Include a printed "solution image" inside the package

Promote as a thoughtful, screen-free gift idea

Tags: 🎨 Creative, Gift-Based, 💻 Digital-Optional

Good for kids who: Love art, design, and making fun, hands-on products

Idea 17: Phone Wallpaper Packs

1. What's the Idea?

Design digital wallpaper packs for phones and tablets using Canva, Procreate, or photo editing tools and sell them as downloadable files.

2. Why It Could Work

Everyone wants their phone to look unique. Cute, inspiring, or funny wallpapers are easy to sell and cost almost nothing to make.

3. Who Might Be Your Customer?

- Friends and classmates
- Teens who love customizing their phones
- Online shoppers looking for digital downloads

4. Steps to Get Started (and Budget)

Estimated Startup Budget: Under $10

- Use free design tools like Canva or apps like Procreate
- Make 5–10 wallpapers per pack

- Save in common phone sizes (1080x1920, etc.)
- Sell as digital downloads through Etsy or Gumroad (with parent help)
- Promote on social media or school flyers with a QR code

5. Pro Tips

- Create collections (e.g., "Positive Vibes," "Ocean Aesthetic")
- Offer custom name versions for extra $$
- Include both light and dark mode versions

Tags: Digital Design, Creative, Low Budget

Good for kids who: Like graphic design, phone art, and tech-savvy creativity

Idea 18: Build Your Own App

1. What's the Idea?

Create an app that solves a small problem or makes life easier for your friends, family, or school. It could be something fun (like a daily joke app), useful (like a homework tracker), or community-focused (like a lost-and-found tool for your neighborhood). You can use no-code platforms to build it—even without knowing how to code!

2. Why It Could Work

Everyone uses apps—and even small, simple apps can be helpful or go viral. With free tools like **Bubble**, **Replit**, **Glide**, or **Bolt.new**, it's easier than ever to turn your ideas into real working apps. Some of today's biggest startups started from ideas like these!

3. Who Might Be Your Customer?

- Classmates or teachers at your school
- Local businesses or community groups
- Friends and family who want a simpler way to do something

4. Steps to Get Started (and Budget)

Estimated Startup Budget: Free–$20

- Think about a small problem people around you face
- Sketch out a simple idea or screen flow for an app that could help
- Use a tool like **Glide**, **Bubble.io**, **Replit.com**, or **Thunkable** to start building
- Share with a few people to test it and give feedback
- If people like it, polish it further—or ask a developer for help later

5. Pro Tips

- Start simple—your first version doesn't need to be perfect
- Ask friends what bugs them most during the day (that's your clue!)
- Create apps for very specific groups (like "Lunch Menu Vote App for 5th Grade")
- Use social media or school flyers to promote and get more users

Tags: 💻 Digital Product, ⚙ Problem-Solving, Startup-Inspired

Good for kids who: Like problem-solving, technology, and making things people actually use

Idea 19: DIY Greeting Cards

1. What's the Idea?

Design and sell your own handmade or printable greeting cards for holidays, birthdays, or school events.

2. Why It Could Work

Cards are thoughtful and always needed for special occasions. A kid-made card is often more meaningful than a store-bought one.

3. Who Might Be Your Customer?

- Parents and grandparents
- Teachers or school staff
- Friends buying gifts for each other

4. Steps to Get Started (and Budget)

Estimated Startup Budget: Under $20

- Use card stock and art supplies or design digitally
- Make 5–10 card themes (birthday, thank you, congratulations)

- Package as singles or in sets
- Price at $2–$4 each
- Sell at school events or online (with parent help)

5. Pro Tips

- Offer blank-inside versions so buyers can write their own notes
- Include envelopes or bundle with bookmarks or stickers
- Make "custom message" cards for extra income

Tags: Creative, Gift-Friendly, Low Budget

Good for kids who: Like drawing, writing, and making people smile

Idea 20: Balloon Animal Party Service

1. What's the Idea?

Learn how to make balloon animals and offer your services at birthday parties or school carnivals.

2. Why It Could Work

Balloon animals are a hit at every kids' party. With practice and some flair, this service can stand out as fun and interactive.

3. Who Might Be Your Customer?

- Parents planning birthday parties
- School event organizers
- Community festivals or family fairs

4. Steps to Get Started (and Budget)

Estimated Startup Budget: $20–$40

- Buy long twisting balloons and a balloon pump
- Learn 5–10 basic shapes (dog, sword, hat, flower) via YouTube

- Create a "menu" of options with pictures
- Offer 30–60 minute party packages
- Advertise through flyers, word of mouth, or online (with parent help)

5. Pro Tips

- Dress up for parties or wear a fun "Balloon Artist" apron
- Hand out small business cards or coloring pages to guests
- Practice ahead so your balloons don't pop mid-show!

Tags: Performance, Event-Friendly, Moderate Budget

Good for kids who: Enjoy entertaining, performing, and making people laugh

Idea 21: Homemade Cookie Kits

1. What's the Idea?

Put together cookie kits with pre-measured dry ingredients and instructions so people can bake fresh cookies at home.

2. Why It Could Work

People love warm cookies but may not have all the ingredients or time to measure. A ready-to-bake kit is fun, tasty, and giftable.

3. Who Might Be Your Customer?

- Busy parents
- People buying gifts or party favors
- Kids and teens who enjoy baking at home

4. Steps to Get Started (and Budget)

Estimated Startup Budget: $15–$30

- Choose a simple cookie recipe (like chocolate chip)
- Pre-measure dry ingredients and seal in bags or jars

- Include clear baking instructions
- Package with ribbon or a custom label
- Source attractive looking containers
- Sell as single kits or holiday bundles

5. Pro Tips

- Add optional mix-ins like M&Ms, marshmallows, or sprinkles
- Offer themed kits for birthdays, holidays, or "just because" gifts
- Be sure to list allergens (like nuts, gluten) clearly

Tags: Creative, Food-Based, Gift-Friendly

Good for kids who: Enjoy baking, giving gifts, and making people smile

Idea 22: Reusable Shopping Bag Art

1. What's the Idea?

Decorate plain canvas or fabric shopping bags with your own artwork and sell them as eco-friendly alternatives to plastic bags.

2. Why It Could Work

Reusable bags are good for the planet, and custom art makes them stylish. They're useful, practical, and perfect for school or grocery runs.

3. Who Might Be Your Customer?

- Parents and teachers
- Farmers market shoppers
- Friends and neighbors

4. Steps to Get Started (and Budget)

Estimated Startup Budget: $20–$40

- Buy blank canvas or cotton tote bags in bulk

- Decorate with fabric paint, stencils, or iron-on designs
- Let dry completely and add a brand label or tag
- Sell at school, events, or online (with adult help)
- Price around $5–$12 depending on size and design

5. Pro Tips

- Offer themed bags (e.g., "Dog Mom Tote" or "Book Lover Bag")
- Create matching sets for families or classrooms
- Promote as gift-ready and eco-friendly

Tags: Creative, Eco-Friendly, Moderate Budget

Good for kids who: Like art, sustainability, and making useful gifts

Idea 23: Toy Cleaning & Repair Service

1. What's the Idea?

Offer to clean or gently repair used toys for parents who want to donate or freshen them up for younger kids.

2. Why It Could Work

Toys get dirty or need a little love before being reused. Many parents would pay a few dollars to have them cleaned, especially before gifting or donating.

3. Who Might Be Your Customer?

- Parents and grandparents
- Babysitters or daycare centers
- Neighbors preparing toys for donation

4. Steps to Get Started (and Budget)

Estimated Startup Budget: Under $20

- Use gentle cleaners, cloths, and magic erasers

- Offer a simple checklist: wipe, sanitize, freshen up
- Create a flyer or list of services with prices ($1–$5 per toy)
- Offer pickup/drop-off (with adult help) or bring to school events
- Use before-and-after photos to build trust

5. Pro Tips

- Offer a flat-rate "toy box refresh" (e.g., 10 toys for $20)
- Specialize in certain toys (e.g., stuffed animals, plastic toys)
- Wear gloves and keep everything safe and sanitary

Tags: Service-Based, Helping Hands, Low Budget

Good for kids who: Like cleaning, organizing, and helping others

Idea 24: DIY Bead Jewelry

1. What's the Idea?

Design and make bead jewelry like necklaces, bracelets, and rings, then sell them in sets or as custom orders.

2. Why It Could Work

Jewelry is personal, wearable, and easy to sell at school events, parties, or online. People love getting handmade accessories—especially from a young creator!

3. Who Might Be Your Customer?

- Friends and classmates
- Parents and teachers buying gifts
- Local shoppers at events or fairs

4. Steps to Get Started (and Budget)

Estimated Startup Budget: $15–$40

- Buy beads, string, clasps, and pliers (starter kits are available

online)
- Make samples with fun color combos or themes
- Price between $3–$10 per piece
- Offer custom name or initial options
- Display in small gift boxes or on a felt board

5. Pro Tips

- Make matching sets (e.g., necklace + bracelet)
- Host a "pop-up shop" at school or a craft fair
- Include a card with your brand name and care instructions

Tags: Creative, Fashion-Friendly, Moderate Budget

Good for kids who: Enjoy jewelry, crafts, and building their own mini brand

Idea 25: Kid-to-Kid Tutoring

1. What's the Idea?

Offer tutoring or homework help to younger kids in subjects you're good at—like math, reading, spelling, or science. Or potentially find several students who can help with different subjects and build a roster of tutoring talent. Earn a commission for every tutoring session.

2. Why It Could Work

Sometimes kids learn better from other kids! Parents love finding a trustworthy, school-smart student who can help their younger child understand something better.

3. Who Might Be Your Customer?

- Families in your school or neighborhood
- Teachers who recommend peer helpers
- Friends with younger siblings

4. Steps to Get Started (and Budget)

Estimated Startup Budget: Free or under $10

- Pick the subjects or grade levels you're confident in
- Offer 20–30 minute tutoring sessions
- Make a flyer or ask teachers for referrals
- Set a simple price ($5–$10 per session)
- Meet in safe places like libraries or online (with parent help)

5. Pro Tips

- Make it fun with flashcards, games, or coloring
- Create a loyalty deal (e.g., 5 sessions for $40)
- Ask for testimonials or parent feedback

Tags: Educational, Helping Hands, Free/Low Budget

Good for kids who: Like helping others, doing schoolwork, and being a positive role model

Idea 26: DIY Magnet Sets

1. What's the Idea?

Make and sell custom magnets using art, photos, or fun sayings. You can design them digitally or make them by hand.

2. Why It Could Work

Magnets are small, collectible, and fun to decorate lockers, fridges, or whiteboards. Custom sets make great gifts or school spirit items.

3. Who Might Be Your Customer?

- Students decorating lockers
- Parents looking for small gifts
- Teachers for classroom use

4. Steps to Get Started (and Budget)

Estimated Startup Budget: $15–$30

- Buy magnetic sheets or plain magnets with adhesive
- Create designs using Canva, markers, or collage

- Cut out and seal (optional with laminate or Mod Podge)
- Package in sets (3–5 per pack)
- Price around $3–$6 per set

5. Pro Tips

- Offer name personalization or initials
- Create themed sets (e.g., food, animals, school mascots)
- Market them as "Locker Decor Kits" or "Fridge Fun Packs"

Tags: Creative, School-Friendly, Moderate Budget

Good for kids who: Like crafts, design, and small collectible items

Idea 27: Digital Coloring Pages

1. What's the Idea?

Design your own coloring pages using drawings, doodles, or digital art. You can sell them as downloadable activity packs or turn them into full-on coloring books using print-on-demand tools like Amazon KDP.

2. Why It Could Work

Parents, teachers, and kids are always looking for fun, screen-free activities. Coloring pages are simple to make, and with no inventory needed, this business can scale easily.

3. Who Might Be Your Customer?

- Parents with young kids
- Teachers and daycare centers
- Birthday gift buyers or party hosts

4. Steps to Get Started (and Budget)
Estimated Startup Budget: Free–$25

- Draw 10–20 coloring pages using paper or a tablet (Canva, Procreate, etc.)
- Save as high-quality PDFs or PNGs
- Option 1: Bundle pages and sell on Etsy or Gumroad (with adult help)
- Option 2: Format as a full coloring book and publish on Amazon KDP
- Price based on format and size ($2–$10)

5. Pro Tips

- Use fun themes: animals, holidays, space, silly monsters
- Offer personalized versions with names
- Add bonus puzzles, mazes, or jokes to stand out
- Promote with flyers, social media, or at school events

Tags: 🎨 Creative, 🖥 Digital or Print, 💵 Low Budget

Good for kids who: Love drawing, storytelling, or making things other kids will enjoy

Idea 28: Seasonal Door Hangers

1. What's the Idea?

Design and sell door hangers for holidays, birthdays, or everyday fun. These can be painted wood, laminated paper, or printable signs.

2. Why It Could Work

People love decorating for the seasons, and a cute door hanger is an easy, affordable way to add fun to a home or classroom.

3. Who Might Be Your Customer?

- Parents and teachers
- Kids wanting room decor
- Holiday shoppers

4. Steps to Get Started (and Budget)

Estimated Startup Budget: $15–$40

- Use cardboard, cardstock, or thin wood
- Paint or decorate with themed phrases (e.g., "Welcome Fall!")

- Add ribbon or hooks
- Price at $3–$10 depending on material
- Sell at school events or online with help

5. Pro Tips

- Make birthday or "Do Not Disturb – Gaming" hangers
- Offer classroom packs for teachers
- Use stencils or stamps to save time

Tags: Creative, Seasonal, Moderate Budget

Good for kids who: Like holidays, crafts, and making fun home décor

Idea 29: Recipe Booklet for Kids

1. What's the Idea?

Write and sell a small collection of kid-friendly recipes you've tested, such as smoothies, snacks, or beginner dinners.

2. Why It Could Work

Other kids want to learn how to cook! A fun, easy-to-follow booklet written by a fellow kid is relatable, useful, and giftable.

3. Who Might Be Your Customer?

- Families with younger kids
- Teachers for classroom giveaways
- Parents looking for gift bundles

4. Steps to Get Started (and Budget)

Estimated Startup Budget: Under $20

- Choose and test 5–10 easy recipes
- Type them up and design pages (use Canva or Google Docs)

- Print and staple into booklets or sell as PDFs
- Price at $3–$8 depending on size and format
- Sell in person or with adult help online
- Setup Amazon KDP account and self publish your book on Amazon

5. Pro Tips

- Include a "shopping list" section and kitchen safety tips
- Add fun drawings or doodles
- Offer themed editions (e.g., "Snack Attack" or "Sleepover Recipes")

Tags: Educational, Food-Based, Low Budget

Good for kids who: Love cooking, writing, or teaching others how to learn

Idea 30: Online Book Club Host

1. What's the Idea?

Start a small online book club where kids can read the same book and meet virtually (with adult help) to talk about it.

2. Why It Could Work

Many kids love to read but don't have anyone to talk about books with. A fun, kid-led club can make reading social and exciting.

3. Who Might Be Your Customer?

- Kids in your grade or neighborhood
- Homeschool families
- Parents looking for enrichment activities

4. Steps to Get Started (and Budget)

Estimated Startup Budget: Free or under $10

- Pick a short, fun book to start with
- Make a flyer or ask your teacher to share

- Host short Zoom or Google Meet sessions (with adult help)
- Ask simple questions and let kids talk about their favorite parts
- Offer club memberships or weekly sessions for a small fee ($3–$5 per meeting)

5. Pro Tips

- Include a printable reading log or coloring page
- Host themed sessions (e.g., "pajama book night")
- Keep it casual, fun, and encouraging

Tags: Educational, Digital Service, Free/Low Budget

Good for kids who: Love reading, leading conversations, and building community

Idea 31: DIY Bird Feeders

1. What's the Idea?

Make homemade bird feeders from recycled or natural materials and sell them as garden or window decorations.

2. Why It Could Work

People enjoy watching birds, especially in their own backyard. A simple, handmade feeder is fun, helpful to nature, and giftable.

3. Who Might Be Your Customer?

- Parents or grandparents
- Teachers (for classroom nature projects)
- Neighbors with yards or balconies

4. Steps to Get Started (and Budget)

Estimated Startup Budget: Under $20

- Use items like pinecones, toilet paper rolls, or wooden spoons
- Roll or cover with peanut butter and bird seed (wear gloves!)

- Package in paper bags or recycled containers
- Add a tag explaining how to hang it
- Price at $3–$6 each depending on size and materials

5. Pro Tips

- Offer a "build-it-yourself" version as a kit
- Label safe usage and storage instructions
- Partner with a local nature center or school garden

Tags: Eco-Friendly, Outdoorsy, Low Budget

Good for kids who: Like animals, crafting, and helping nature

Idea 32: Birthday Party Box

1. What's the Idea?

Create and sell themed birthday party boxes with decorations, games, and favors all in one package.

2. Why It Could Work

Parents love convenience. A pre-packed birthday kit makes it easier to host a party without shopping at multiple places.

3. Who Might Be Your Customer?

- Busy parents
- Gift givers looking for something different
- Party planners or friends of the birthday kid

4. Steps to Get Started (and Budget)

Estimated Startup Budget: $30−$75

- Choose a theme (e.g., dinosaurs, unicorns, space)
- Include balloons, signs, activity ideas, and small prizes

- Package in a sturdy box with a fun label
- Price around $20–$40 depending on what's inside
- Promote via word of mouth, flyers, or parent groups (with adult help)

5. Pro Tips

- Offer add-ons like cupcakes, stickers, or a music playlist
- Include "Host Tips" inside the box
- Create "mini kits" for smaller parties or classrooms

Tags: Event-Based, Creative, Moderate/High Budget

Good for kids who: Enjoy organizing, birthdays, and party planning

Idea 33: Custom Name Signs

1. What's the Idea?

Make personalized name signs for bedrooms, desks, or lockers using wood, cardboard, or foam board.

2. Why It Could Work

Kids love seeing their names on things. A custom sign is fun, decorative, and can be themed to match hobbies or favorite colors.

3. Who Might Be Your Customer?

- Friends or classmates
- Parents buying gifts
- Teachers for name tags or class décor

4. Steps to Get Started (and Budget)

Estimated Startup Budget: $15–$40

- Use sturdy materials (wood cutouts, foam board, or thick paper)
- Decorate with paint, markers, glitter, or stickers

161

- Offer a few font or color options
- Price at $5–$15 depending on size and detail
- Take custom orders through a printed order form or digital form (with parent help)

5. Pro Tips

- Make samples with common names to show off
- Offer themed signs (e.g., "Gamer Zone – Ethan")
- Add hanging hardware or magnets to the back

Tags: Creative, Gift-Friendly, Moderate Budget

Good for kids who: Enjoy decorating, personalization, and making others feel special

Idea 34: Homework Checklist Templates

1. What's the Idea?

Design printable or reusable homework checklists and sell them as tools to help kids stay organized.

2. Why It Could Work

Many kids struggle with school organization. A colorful, kid-made checklist feels relatable and helpful—especially when it's reusable or printable.

3. Who Might Be Your Customer?

- Students
- Parents helping with school routines
- Teachers looking for tools for their classroom

4. Steps to Get Started (and Budget)

Estimated Startup Budget: Under $10

- Design templates in Google Docs, Canva, or by hand

- Include boxes for subjects, reminders, and goals
- Save as printable PDFs or laminate for reuse
- Sell as printed sheets, digital downloads, or laminated versions
- Price at $2–$6 depending on the format

5. Pro Tips

- Offer versions by grade level or subject
- Create bonus tools like "Study Tracker" or "Test Countdown" pages
- Add your logo or business name in the footer

Tags: Educational, Digital/Printable, Low Budget

Good for kids who: Like school success tools, organizing, and design

Idea 35: Pet-Sitting and/or Dog Walking

1. What's the Idea?

Offer to care for pets while neighbors are away or walk their dogs after school (with parent approval and help when needed).

2. Why It Could Work

Pet owners want someone they trust. A helpful neighborhood kid is more affordable than a professional sitter—and often more flexible.

3. Who Might Be Your Customer?

- Neighbors with busy schedules
- Friends going on vacation
- People with older pets that need extra attention

4. Steps to Get Started (and Budget)

Estimated Startup Budget: Under $10

- Decide what services you're offering (walking, feeding, cleanup)
- Make a flyer or ask neighbors directly

- Set a fair price per walk or per visit
- Keep notes for each pet and communicate with owners clearly
- Track your schedule and repeat clients

5. Pro Tips

- Offer a "Pet Journal" for owners to see updates
- Learn basic pet safety tips ahead of time
- Be punctual, respectful, and gentle with animals

Tags: Animal-Friendly, Helping Hands, Low Budget

Good for kids who: Love pets, enjoy responsibility, and like being outdoors

Idea 36: Digital Vision Boards

1. What's the Idea?

Help people create digital vision boards using Canva or other tools to visualize their goals, dreams, or plans for the year.

2. Why It Could Work

Vision boards are popular with both kids and adults. A digital version is easy to share, update, and save—perfect for staying motivated.

3. Who Might Be Your Customer?

- Students setting goals for school or sports
- Parents or teachers working on self-improvement
- People who love digital design and affirmations

4. Steps to Get Started (and Budget)

Estimated Startup Budget: Under $10

- Use Canva or Google Slides to create sample boards
- Offer custom packages: "Dream Board," "Athlete Goals," "New

Year Reset"
- Create a form to ask what images, words, or goals they want
- Price at $5–$15 depending on customization
- Deliver by email as a downloadable PNG or PDF

5. Pro Tips

- Include an inspiring quote or theme for each board
- Offer a "refresh" service every few months
- Create a few free templates to attract attention

Tags: Digital Design, Motivational, Low Budget

Good for kids who: Like design, positivity, and helping people stay focused

Idea 37: Holiday Yard Sign Rentals

1. What's the Idea?

Create or collect fun yard signs for holidays or birthdays and rent them out to families in your neighborhood.

2. Why It Could Work

People love celebrating but don't want to buy and store big signs. Renting is fun, affordable, and keeps things fresh for every occasion.

3. Who Might Be Your Customer?

- Parents throwing birthday parties
- Neighbors who decorate for holidays
- Schools or local churches hosting events

4. Steps to Get Started (and Budget)

Estimated Startup Budget: $50–$100+

- Buy or make reusable yard signs (Happy Birthday, spooky Halloween, etc.)

- Store safely between uses
- Set a rental price per 24–48 hours (e.g., $10–$25 per rental)
- Promote with flyers or by word of mouth
- Offer delivery, setup, and pickup with adult help

5. Pro Tips

- Bundle signs for holidays or milestone birthdays
- Offer add-ons like balloons or mini chalkboards
- Keep signs clean and weather-protected for reuse

Tags: Event-Based, Seasonal, Higher Budget

Good for kids who: Enjoy parties, decorating, and working outdoors

Idea 38: Personalized Voice Messages

1. What's the Idea?

Record custom audio messages (funny, sweet, or themed) and sell them as birthday surprises, alarms, or motivational quotes.

2. Why It Could Work

People love personalized gifts—especially from a kid! It's a fun way to surprise someone using just your voice and creativity.

3. Who Might Be Your Customer?

- Parents or siblings
- Friends sending birthday messages
- Teachers using them for class rewards

4. Steps to Get Started (and Budget)

Estimated Startup Budget: Free or under $10

- Use your phone, tablet, or computer to record audio
- Offer message types: "Birthday Surprise," "Wake-Up Alarm,"

"Homework Hype"
- Ask what tone or name to include
- Deliver files by email or text
- Price at $3–$7 depending on length/customization

5. Pro Tips

- Create character voices or sing short jingles
- Offer a discount for bundles or recurring customers
- Get permission from adults before recording others

Tags: Digital Product, Creative, Free/Low Budget

Good for kids who: Enjoy performing, recording, or being the voice of fun

Idea 39: Backyard Obstacle Course Setup

1. What's the Idea?

Design and set up temporary obstacle courses for birthday parties or playdates using cones, rope, hula hoops, and other gear. This could also expand to all types of party rental stuff like inflatables and other party rental supplies.

2. Why It Could Work

Active play is always in demand, and parents love off-screen entertainment for kids. You provide fun and movement—without the screens.

3. Who Might Be Your Customer?

- Parents hosting parties or playdates
- Daycare centers or kids' clubs
- PE teachers looking for ideas

4. Steps to Get Started (and Budget)

Estimated Startup Budget: $30–$75

- Buy or borrow basic equipment (cones, jump ropes, pool noodles)
- Create different course types (relay, agility, silly challenge)
- Offer 30–60 minute "event setup and guide" service
- Charge a flat rate per session (e.g., $25–$50)
- Clean and store materials for reuse

5. Pro Tips

- Theme your courses (pirate, ninja, jungle, etc.)
- Offer awards or printable "course finisher" badges
- Work with a parent or older sibling as your co-coach

Tags: Active, Outdoors, Moderate Budget

Good for kids who: Like sports, leading activities, and making others move

Idea 40: Classroom Supply Restocker

1. What's the Idea?

Offer a service to restock and organize classroom supplies like pencils, tissues, markers, and sanitizer.

2. Why It Could Work

Teachers are busy, and classrooms get messy fast. A helpful kid offering a weekly or monthly refresh is a win for everyone.

3. Who Might Be Your Customer?

- Teachers at your school
- Homeschool parents
- Tutors or classroom aides

4. Steps to Get Started (and Budget)

Estimated Startup Budget: Under $15

- Ask teachers what they need and how often
- Create a checklist and inventory tracker

- Use your own supplies or charge for restocking
- Offer weekly or bi-weekly service
- Price depending on time or materials (e.g., $5–$15 per visit)

5. Pro Tips

- Decorate a caddy or organizer to bring each time
- Offer to wipe desks or sharpen pencils as a bonus
- Add a "Thank You Note" with each visit to brighten the teacher's day

Tags: School-Based, Helping Hands, Low Budget

Good for kids who: Like organizing, being helpful, and supporting teachers

Idea 41: Handmade Soap Bars

1. What's the Idea?

Create small bars of handmade soap using natural ingredients, colors, and scents. Sell them as gifts or part of self-care kits.

2. Why It Could Work

Soap is useful, giftable, and fun to make. With the right scents and packaging, you can turn it into a product that feels high-end—even if it's homemade.

3. Who Might Be Your Customer?

- Parents and teachers
- Craft fair shoppers
- Friends buying birthday gifts

4. Steps to Get Started (and Budget)

Estimated Startup Budget: $25–$50

- Use melt-and-pour soap bases (easy and safe with adult help)

- Add essential oils, colors, and dried flowers (optional)
- Pour into molds and let harden
- Wrap in parchment or boxes and add labels
- Sell for $3–$6 per bar depending on size

5. Pro Tips

- Offer "soap bundles" like Lemon + Lavender + Oatmeal
- Create holiday-themed shapes or scents
- Include ingredient info and allergy warnings

Tags: Self-Care, Craft-Based, Moderate Budget

Good for kids who: Love creating gifts, mixing scents, and packaging beautiful things

Idea 42: Sports. Highlights Editor

1. What's the Idea?

Use video editing tools to help teammates or classmates turn game footage into short highlight reels. Also potentially setup video recording for other youth sports to create highlights and youth sports channel on Youtube and or Twitch.

2. Why It Could Work

Many athletes (and their parents) want videos for fun or for school teams—but not everyone knows how to edit. A sports-minded kid with editing skills is a perfect fit.

3. Who Might Be Your Customer?

- Teammates or athletes at school
- Parents of younger players
- Coaches or school sports teams

4. Steps to Get Started (and Budget)

Estimated Startup Budget: Free–$25

- Use editing tools like CapCut, iMovie, or Canva Video
- Ask for game footage and what highlights they want
- Add music, slow-mo, or text overlays
- Price each reel at $10–$30 depending on length and features
- Deliver via USB, email, or Google Drive

5. Pro Tips

- Offer seasonal packages (e.g., "Fall Highlights Reel")
- Include a "hype" intro or outro
- Respect privacy—get permission before posting anywhere

Tags: Digital Service, Sports-Based, Low/Moderate Budget

Good for kids who: Enjoy video editing, sports, and creative story-telling

Idea 43: Recycled Jar Lanterns

1. What's the Idea?

Make glowing lanterns out of recycled jars decorated with paint, tissue paper, or stencils. Sell them as decorations or gifts.

2. Why It Could Work

They're eye-catching, reusable, and make people feel cozy. Great for holidays, nightlights, or outdoor events.

3. Who Might Be Your Customer?

- Parents and neighbors
- Gift shoppers at local events
- Teachers looking for cozy classroom decor

4. Steps to Get Started (and Budget)

Estimated Startup Budget: Under $20

- Collect clean jars (mason jars, spaghetti sauce jars, etc.)
- Decorate with tissue paper, glass paint, or stickers

- Insert LED tealights (safe and long-lasting)
- Package with ribbon or tags
- Price around $5–$10 per lantern

5. Pro Tips

- Make themed versions: fall leaves, winter snowflakes, "Happy Birthday"
- Sell bundles for events (e.g., 3 for $20)
- Include an extra LED light as a bonus

Tags: Creative, Eco-Friendly, Low Budget

Good for kids who: Like upcycling, decorating, and cozy lighting

Idea 44: Personalized Stationery Packs

1. What's the Idea?

Design custom notecards, letterhead, or to-do lists with names, themes, or fun icons. Sell in printable or printed form.

2. Why It Could Work

Kids and adults still love writing notes—and personalized stationery makes it more fun and memorable. A thoughtful, practical gift item.

3. Who Might Be Your Customer?

- Classmates and teachers
- Parents looking for gifts
- Small businesses wanting custom notepads

4. Steps to Get Started (and Budget)

Estimated Startup Budget: $10–$30

- Use Canva or Procreate to create simple, clean designs
- Offer personalization (name, favorite colors, icons)

- Sell as PDFs or printed and packaged in sets
- Price at $5–$15 per pack depending on quantity and format
- Promote through word-of-mouth, flyers, or parent help online

5. Pro Tips

- Include matching envelopes or sticker seals
- Offer digital and printed options
- Create "teacher packs" for appreciation gifts

Tags: Creative, Printable, Gift-Friendly

Good for kids who: Enjoy graphic design, stationery, and personalization

Idea 45: Locker Decor Kits

1. What's the Idea?

Create locker decoration kits with mirrors, magnets, mini posters, and cute accessories that help kids personalize their space at school.

2. Why It Could Work

Lockers are like a mini home base at school. Kids love decorating them—especially when everything comes in one stylish bundle.

3. Who Might Be Your Customer?

- Middle school students
- Parents shopping for back-to-school gifts
- Friends looking for birthday ideas

4. Steps to Get Started (and Budget)

Estimated Startup Budget: $25–$60

- Include mini mirrors, fun magnets, note holders, and small dry-erase boards

- Package everything in a pouch or small box
- Offer color or theme choices (e.g., "Galaxy Kit," "Pastel Power")
- Price between $10–$25 per kit
- Sell at school, online (with adult help), or during back-to-school events

5. Pro Tips

- Offer a "refill" pack with new magnets or notes
- Include a tip sheet: "5 Locker Organization Hacks"
- Personalize with initials or names for extra value

Tags: School-Friendly, Creative, Moderate Budget

Good for kids who: Like style, organization, and school fun

Idea 46: Custom Digital Avatars

1. What's the Idea?

Create cartoon-style or gaming-inspired digital avatars for people to use as profile pictures, gamer icons, or social media images.

2. Why It Could Work

Everyone online wants a fun or cool profile pic. A custom avatar stands out—and if it's made by a kid, it can feel extra unique and relatable.

3. Who Might Be Your Customer?

- Friends on gaming platforms or social media
- Tweens and teens who want cool profile pics
- Streamers or content creators starting out

4. Steps to Get Started (and Budget)

Estimated Startup Budget: Free or under $20

- Use Canva, IbisPaint, Procreate, or other drawing tools
- Offer a few different styles (cartoon, pixel, superhero, etc.)

- Ask for a photo or description and turn it into a custom drawing
- Deliver digital file (PNG or JPG) via email or DM
- Price between $5–$15 per avatar

5. Pro Tips

- Offer bundle deals (e.g., 3 avatars for $20)
- Add optional backgrounds or text
- Keep a style gallery to show your work to new clients

Tags: Digital Design, Tech-Friendly, Low Budget

Good for kids who: Love drawing, gaming, and online creativity

Idea 47: Kid Podcast Host or Producer

1. What's the Idea?

Start a podcast (with adult help) where you talk about fun topics like books, sports, games, or interview other kids and guests. And/or involve a friend and create a podcast with a few speakers.

2. Why It Could Work

Podcasts are popular—and a kid-led one feels fresh, funny, and relatable. You can grow an audience and maybe even get sponsors later on.

3. Who Might Be Your Customer?

- Other kids looking for fun content
- Parents looking for safe, smart shows
- Teachers who want classroom-friendly media

4. Steps to Get Started (and Budget)

Estimated Startup Budget: $0–$50

- Use a phone, tablet, or mic to record
- Choose a theme and brainstorm 5–10 episode ideas
- Edit with free apps like GarageBand or Audacity
- Post on podcast platforms (with adult help)
- Share with your school, friends, and social media

5. Pro Tips

- Keep episodes short (5–15 minutes)
- Invite guests or have a sibling co-host
- End each show with a catchphrase or joke

Tags: Creative, Media-Based, Low/Moderate Budget

Good for kids who: Like talking, performing, and sharing ideas with the world

Idea 48: Temporary Tattoo Designer

1. What's the Idea?

Design fun temporary tattoos—either printable or using tattoo paper—to sell at school events or online.

2. Why It Could Work

Temporary tattoos are cool, easy to wear, and totally customizable. Kids love wearing them at parties, school events, and sports games.

3. Who Might Be Your Customer?

- Kids at parties or school events
- Parents looking for party favors
- Coaches or club leaders ordering team designs

4. Steps to Get Started (and Budget)

Estimated Startup Budget: $20–$50

- Use design tools to create fun images (stars, slogans, mascots)
- Print on temporary tattoo paper or use a print shop

- Package in small sets (3–5 per pack)
- Price at $2–$5 per set
- Sell in person or online with adult help

5. Pro Tips

- Offer custom name or team tattoos
- Create holiday sets (e.g., Halloween or Valentine's Day)
- Include instructions with every pack

Tags: Creative, Fashion-Friendly, Moderate Budget

Good for kids who: Like art, branding, and designing fun stuff people wear

Idea 49: Pet Photo Shoots

1. What's the Idea?

Take cute, funny, or creative photos of pets for their owners—using props, backdrops, or even holiday themes.

2. Why It Could Work

People love their pets and want to capture fun memories. A kid with a good eye for photos and a love for animals can do this affordably.

3. Who Might Be Your Customer?

- Pet owners
- Friends and family with cats or dogs
- Social media–obsessed pet parents

4. Steps to Get Started (and Budget)

Estimated Startup Budget: Free–$30

- Use a smartphone or camera with good lighting
- Create a few DIY backdrops (blankets, poster boards, etc.)

- Offer 15–30 minute photo sessions
- Deliver digital photo sets or 1 printed image
- Charge $5–$20 depending on what's included

5. Pro Tips

- Use treats to keep pets still and happy
- Offer holiday themes like "Santa Paws" or "Pup in the Pumpkin Patch"
- Always get parent help for scheduling and safety

Tags: Pet-Based, Creative, Free/Low Budget

Good for kids who: Love animals, taking pictures, and being patient

Idea 50: Custom "Jar of Jokes" or Affirmations

1. What's the Idea?

Create small jars or containers filled with funny jokes or inspiring affirmations—one per day—to help people smile and feel better.

2. Why It Could Work

These make great desk accessories, gifts, or feel-good purchases. Everyone could use a laugh or a confidence boost each day.

3. Who Might Be Your Customer?

- Teachers for their desks
- Parents as morning pick-me-ups
- Friends giving thoughtful gifts

4. Steps to Get Started (and Budget)

Estimated Startup Budget: Under $20

- Write or print 30–50 short jokes or kind messages

- Fold and fill into jars, tins, or decorated paper boxes
- Label them ("Laugh a Day" or "Daily Confidence Notes")
- Price around $5–$10 depending on size and packaging
- Sell at gift tables, fairs, or school events

5. Pro Tips

- Offer themed versions: "Test Day Boosters" or "Sleepover Laughs"
- Use recycled jars or origami containers
- Include blank slips for customers to add their own

Tags: Creative, Gift-Based, Low Budget

Good for kids who: Love writing, humor, and spreading positivity

Idea 51: Lunchbox Notes Business

1. What's the Idea?

Create packs of fun, inspiring, or silly lunchbox notes that parents can tuck into their kids' lunches each day.

2. Why It Could Work

Parents love simple ways to connect with their kids. These pre-made notes save time and add a thoughtful surprise to lunch.

3. Who Might Be Your Customer?

- Parents of younger kids
- Teachers using notes for rewards
- Gift buyers looking for something different

4. Steps to Get Started (and Budget)

Estimated Startup Budget: Under $20

- Write or print 20–40 unique notes per pack (jokes, affirmations, reminders)

- Use colorful paper or add cute borders
- Package in envelopes or boxes
- Price each pack at $4–$8
- Sell in person, at school events, or online with parent help

5. Pro Tips

- Create themed sets: jokes, holidays, test day encouragement
- Offer a digital printable version too
- Include blank ones for parents to write their own

Tags: Gift-Based, Creative, Low Budget

Good for kids who: Love writing, jokes, and spreading joy

Idea 52: DIY Face Mask Kits (Skincare)

1. What's the Idea?

Make skincare kits with natural ingredients for homemade face masks—great for sleepovers, birthdays, or self-care gifts.

2. Why It Could Work

Face masks are a popular part of teen self-care. A DIY kit makes the experience fun and feel special.

3. Who Might Be Your Customer?

- Teens or tweens at sleepovers
- Gift shoppers
- Parents planning spa-themed birthdays

4. Steps to Get Started (and Budget)

Estimated Startup Budget: $20–$50

- Choose a few recipes (e.g., oatmeal honey, banana mash)
- Pre-measure dry ingredients into small containers

- Include mixing instructions and optional extras (headbands, spoons)
- Sell kits for $6–$12
- Package nicely in spa-style pouches or gift boxes

5. Pro Tips

- Offer "refill packs" with just the ingredients
- Emphasize natural and gentle ingredients
- Add mini stickers or scent options

Tags: Self-Care, Beauty, Moderate Budget

Good for kids who: Like skincare, packaging gifts, and wellness trends

Idea 53: Comic Strip Subscriptions

1. What's the Idea?

Write and draw a weekly or monthly comic strip that people can subscribe to digitally or get as a printed version.

2. Why It Could Work

If it's funny or relatable, people will look forward to your comic. This is a great way to grow a loyal fan base—especially among classmates.

3. Who Might Be Your Customer?

- Friends and family
- Teachers using it for class reading time
- Online fans who love comics

4. Steps to Get Started (and Budget)

Estimated Startup Budget: Free–$20

- Draw 3–5 comic episodes as a starter set
- Choose whether to publish weekly, bi-weekly, or monthly

- Offer email delivery, a private webpage, or physical printouts
- Price at $1–$3/month or $5–$10 for a printed pack
- Promote by sharing previews or funny moments

5. Pro Tips

- Include a "character spotlight" or bonus sketch each month
- Offer a custom comic for extra income
- Ask for reader feedback to improve your stories

Tags: Creative, Digital or Print, Low Budget

Good for kids who: Love storytelling, drawing, and humor

Idea 54: Personalized Water Bottles

1. What's the Idea?

Design and decorate reusable water bottles with names, stickers, or vinyl decals to make each one unique.

2. Why It Could Work

Water bottles are used daily—and personalization helps kids keep track of theirs while adding style.

3. Who Might Be Your Customer?

- Students at school
- Parents looking for gifts
- Coaches or teams ordering in bulk

4. Steps to Get Started (and Budget)

Estimated Startup Budget: $30–$75

- Buy blank bottles or ask buyers to provide their own
- Use waterproof vinyl, decals, or paint pens

- Offer name, initials, icons (sports, animals, etc.)
- Price at $8–$15 per bottle
- Package with care instructions and optional tag

5. Pro Tips

- Offer matching bags or stickers
- Create a "Team Pack" bundle
- Use outdoor vinyl or Mod Podge for long-lasting results

Tags: Practical, Customizable, Moderate Budget

Good for kids who: Like crafts, personalization, and useful gifts

Idea 55: Babysitter Bag Creator

1. What's the Idea?

Build fun "Babysitter Bags" filled with games, coloring pages, books, or crafts for kids to use during babysitting gigs.

2. Why It Could Work

Babysitters who bring their own bag of fun are seen as pros. Parents love it, and sitters enjoy having pre-planned activities.

3. Who Might Be Your Customer?

- Tweens and teens who babysit
- Parents buying a kit for their babysitter
- Aspiring babysitters preparing to get hired

4. Steps to Get Started (and Budget)

Estimated Startup Budget: $20–$40

- Choose 5–8 easy, mess-free activities
- Include books, coloring sheets, small toys, and instructions

- Package in a reusable tote
- Price each bag between $15–$25
- Offer refills or themed add-ons (e.g., rainy day, holidays)

5. Pro Tips

- Include a log sheet for tracking what kids liked
- Offer versions by age group (toddlers vs. older kids)
- Add a "Babysitter Tips" card for bonus value

Tags: Practical, Service Support, Moderate Budget

Good for kids who: Want to babysit, enjoy planning activities, or love working with children

Idea 56: "Clean My Backpack" Service

1. What's the Idea?

Offer to clean, organize, and refresh kids' messy backpacks—removing crumbs, trash, old papers, and organizing supplies.

2. Why It Could Work

Backpacks get messy fast. Parents and kids appreciate someone helping keep school stuff clean and organized.

3. Who Might Be Your Customer?

- Classmates
- Parents of younger students
- Teachers for student reward days

4. Steps to Get Started (and Budget)

Estimated Startup Budget: Under $10

- Make a checklist for what's included (wiping down, sorting, restocking)

- Offer the service at lunch or after school with parent/teacher permission
- Set a simple rate ($3–$8 per bag)
- Bring a small kit: wipes, trash bag, zip pouches
- Offer monthly memberships or repeat visit discounts

5. Pro Tips

- Include a thank-you note or organization tips
- Offer extra add-ons like "pencil restock" or "planner setup"
- Respect personal space—ask before tossing anything

Tags: School-Friendly, Service-Based, Low Budget

Good for kids who: Like cleaning, organizing, and being helpful

Idea 57: Custom Playlist Curator

1. What's the Idea?

Make personalized music playlists for birthdays, parties, studying, or relaxing—based on someone's favorite artists or mood.

2. Why It Could Work

Kids and teens love music. A curated playlist saves them time and feels more personal than just using random mixes.

3. Who Might Be Your Customer?

- Friends who love music
- People planning parties or road trips
- Students looking for study playlists

4. Steps to Get Started (and Budget)

Estimated Startup Budget: Free

- Ask questions (favorite artists, mood, type of playlist)
- Use Spotify, YouTube, or Apple Music (check platform rules)

- Create and name the playlist
- Send via link or QR code
- Price at $3–$10 depending on length or number of playlists

5. Pro Tips

- Offer themed bundles ("Rainy Day," "Basketball Warm-Up," "Road Trip")
- Add a fun digital cover image
- Keep music school-appropriate if needed

Tags: Digital Product, Creative, Free Budget

Good for kids who: Love music, curation, and creating a vibe

Idea 58: Room Re-Organizer for Kids

1. What's the Idea?

Help other kids clean and reorganize their rooms—moving furniture, sorting toys, and refreshing the space.Also use some of the new AI tools to help visualize a better way to setup a kid's room to optimize space.You would essentially be providing room consulting.

2. Why It Could Work

Kids are more likely to listen to another kid. Many rooms get cluttered fast, and having help makes it feel less overwhelming.

3. Who Might Be Your Customer?

- Friends and classmates
- Parents hiring help for their kids
- Siblings teaming up

4. Steps to Get Started (and Budget)

Estimated Startup Budget: Free or under $10

- Offer a free mini consult to walk through the space
- Create zones (reading, toys, clothes) and label bins
- Use checklists and organize in sessions (1–2 hours)
- Price per session ($10–$25 depending on time)
- Get parent approval and supervision

5. Pro Tips

- Use printed labels or color coding
- Bring a small kit with stickers, folders, or zip bags
- Offer follow-up visits or maintenance plans

Tags: Service-Based, Organizing, Low Budget

Good for kids who: Like home design, helping friends, and transforming spaces

Idea 59: DIY Lip Balm Business

1. What's the Idea?

Make and sell your own lip balm in small containers, using natural oils, waxes, and flavors. Various small charms can be added/connected to the lip balms for a prettier look.

2. Why It Could Work

Lip balm is useful year-round, easy to make, and fun to customize with scents, shimmer, or colors.

3. Who Might Be Your Customer?

- Students
- Parents buying gifts or stocking stuffers
- Friends hosting sleepovers or birthday parties

4. Steps to Get Started (and Budget)

Estimated Startup Budget: $25–$50

- Use beeswax, coconut oil, and flavor oils

- Melt ingredients with adult help and pour into small tins or tubes
- Label and decorate each product
- Price at $2–$5 each
- Sell in bundles, gift sets, or spa party packs

5. Pro Tips

- Offer custom labels for birthdays or holidays
- Add shimmer or tinted options
- Be sure to follow basic safety and cleanliness guidelines

Tags: Beauty, Craft-Based, Moderate Budget

Good for kids who: Like skincare, DIY products, and branding

Idea 60: Local Guide for Kids

1. What's the Idea?

Create a short guide for your town or neighborhood listing kid-friendly places to visit—like the best parks, ice cream spots, and activity centers.

2. Why It Could Work

Parents are always looking for fun ideas. A "kid's guide to [your city]" gives families a new way to explore with insider tips.

3. Who Might Be Your Customer?

- Families new to your area
- Local schools, camps, or libraries
- Tourists looking for family fun

4. Steps to Get Started (and Budget)

Estimated Startup Budget: Free–$20

- Visit and review 5–10 fun spots in your area

- Add short write-ups, photos, and favorite picks
- Format in Canva or Google Docs as a printable or PDF
- Sell digital downloads ($3–$5) or printed booklets ($5–$10)
- Offer updates or seasonal editions

5. Pro Tips

- Include a "Top 5" list, coupons, or scavenger hunt
- Collaborate with local shops or businesses
- Offer a free sample page to attract buyers

Tags: Educational, Local-Based, Low Budget

Good for kids who: Know their city, like writing, and love sharing adventures

Idea 61: Emoji Poster Prints

1. What's the Idea?

Design and print funny or expressive posters using emoji-style art or text. Sell them for locker decorations, room decor, or gifts.

2. Why It Could Work

Kids love emojis, and posters are a fun, affordable way to personalize a space. A clever or funny design can become a popular item.

3. Who Might Be Your Customer?

- Classmates
- Teachers decorating classrooms
- Parents looking for low-cost gifts

4. Steps to Get Started (and Budget)

Estimated Startup Budget: $10–$30

- Design posters in Canva, Google Docs, or draw by hand
- Include catchy phrases or popular emojis

- Print on thick paper and package in clear sleeves
- Price at $3–$7 each
- Sell at school, fairs, or online (with adult help)

5. Pro Tips

- Offer "locker-size" mini posters or full-size wall versions
- Use bright, bold fonts for maximum effect
- Sell bundles (e.g., 3 for $10)

Tags: Creative, School-Friendly, Low/Moderate Budget

Good for kids who: Like design, humor, and making people smile

Idea 62: Pen Pal Stationery Sets

1. What's the Idea?

Make themed sets of pen pal stationery with matching paper, envelopes, and stickers—perfect for kids who love writing letters.

2. Why It Could Work

Pen pals are making a comeback. A cute stationery set makes writing fun, and it encourages reading, writing, and connection.

3. Who Might Be Your Customer?

- Kids with pen pals
- Parents or teachers promoting letter-writing
- Gift buyers

4. Steps to Get Started (and Budget)

Estimated Startup Budget: $10–$30

- Design themed pages and envelopes
- Include 5–10 letter pages, stickers, and matching envelopes

- Package in a folder or clear sleeve
- Price at $5–$10 per set
- Sell at school, libraries, or online (with adult help)

5. Pro Tips

- Offer holiday, animal, or hobby themes
- Include a card with "10 fun questions to ask your pen pal"
- Add a mini stamp tracker or address book page

Tags: Creative, Educational, Low/Moderate Budget

Good for kids who: Love writing, connecting, and cute designs

Idea 63: Tech Helper for Seniors

1. What's the Idea?

Offer a service where you help older adults with simple technology problems—like how to use email, set up a phone and/or any apps, fix a printer, or organize files and photos.

2. Why It Could Work

Many older people struggle with everyday tech. They often don't want to call a company or wait on hold—they'd rather get help from someone patient and friendly (like you!).

3. Who Might Be Your Customer?

- Grandparents or neighbors
- Older adults in your community
- Seniors at churches, libraries, or retirement communities

4. Steps to Get Started (and Budget)

Estimated Startup Budget: Free–$15

- Create a flyer offering "Tech Help for Seniors"
- List things you can help with (email, apps, passwords, Zoom, etc.)
- Offer short 20–30 minute sessions
- Charge $5–$15 depending on the task and time
- Ask for referrals or offer a free first session

5. Pro Tips

- Always explain things slowly and clearly
- Bring a checklist of common tasks so you stay organized
- Offer printed "how-to" cards to leave behind
- Be patient and respectful—this builds trust and loyalty

Tags: Service-Based, Tech-Friendly, Low Budget

Good for kids who: Are good with phones or computers, enjoy teaching others, and like helping people feel confident

Idea 64: Reading Reward Tracker Kits

1. What's the Idea?

Create kits that help kids track their reading progress and earn rewards—great for summer, school, or personal goals.

2. Why It Could Work

Parents and teachers want kids to read more. A tracker makes the process visual, exciting, and goal-driven.

3. Who Might Be Your Customer?

- Parents encouraging reading at home
- Teachers for reading challenges
- Libraries or reading groups

4. Steps to Get Started (and Budget)

Estimated Startup Budget: Under $20

- Create printable charts, bookmarks, and goal cards
- Include stickers or mini reward slips

- Package in folders or envelopes
- Price at $4–$8 per kit
- Sell at school, libraries, or online with adult help

5. Pro Tips

- Offer "Custom Name" tracker kits
- Include fun categories like "Fantasy Books," "Comics," "Poetry"
- Add a checklist with milestones (e.g., "Read 10 books = Prize!")

Tags: Educational, Printable, Low Budget

Good for kids who: Love reading, setting goals, and helping others build good habits

Idea 65: Greeting Video Service

1. What's the Idea?

Record personalized video greetings for birthdays, holidays, congratulations, or encouragement—delivered by email or text.

2. Why It Could Work

A video feels more special than a text. People love sending fun surprises, and a kid-made video adds charm and humor.

3. Who Might Be Your Customer?

- Parents and grandparents
- Friends sending birthday wishes
- Teachers for classroom celebrations

4. Steps to Get Started (and Budget)

Estimated Startup Budget: Free–$10

- Offer message types: birthday, pep talk, congratulations, etc.
- Use a phone or webcam to record short, upbeat messages

- Personalize with names, hobbies, or jokes
- Deliver via email, Google Drive, or a private link
- Price each message at $3–$8

5. Pro Tips

- Wear fun outfits or use props
- Use a whiteboard or signs for visual flair
- Get permission before using names in public videos

Tags: Digital Product, Creative, Free/Low Budget

Good for kids who: Love performing, speaking, and cheering others up

Idea 66: Local Nature Guide for Kids

1. What's the Idea?

Create a kid-friendly guide to local plants, animals, or hiking spots with fun facts, drawings, or photos.This could potentially be an app or a website and/or newsletter.

2. Why It Could Work

Many kids enjoy exploring outdoors. A guide written by another kid makes nature feel more fun, relatable, and cool.

3. Who Might Be Your Customer?

- Families who enjoy hikes and nature walks
- Teachers and summer camps
- Local parks or libraries

4. Steps to Get Started (and Budget)

Estimated Startup Budget: Free–$20

- Explore local parks or neighborhoods with an adult

- Take notes, photos, or draw what you find
- Write short descriptions or add fun facts
- Format into a PDF or print booklet
- Sell for $3–$10 depending on format

5. Pro Tips

- Include a scavenger hunt or checklist
- Offer seasonal updates or new editions
- Add safety tips for outdoor adventures

Tags: Educational, Nature-Based, Low Budget

Good for kids who: Love the outdoors, writing, and teaching others

Idea 67: Joke of the Day Subscription

1. What's the Idea?

Send subscribers one funny, clean, kid-approved joke every day by email or text message.

2. Why It Could Work

Everyone loves to laugh—and parents love safe, fun content that makes their kids smile daily.

3. Who Might Be Your Customer?

- Kids with phones
- Parents who want to brighten their kids' day
- Teachers who want a daily class opener

4. Steps to Get Started (and Budget)

Estimated Startup Budget: Free–$10

- Write or collect 30–60 clean, original jokes
- Offer delivery via email, text, or Google Classroom

- Charge a subscription ($1–$3/month)
- Add personalization (e.g., "Hey Ava, today's joke is…")
- Promote to families, teachers, or youth groups

5. Pro Tips

- Create bonus joke packs or themed joke weeks
- Add illustrations or emojis
- Keep jokes short and easy to read out loud

Tags: Creative, Digital, Free/Low Budget

Good for kids who: Enjoy comedy, writing, and spreading happiness

Idea 68: Mini Travel Journal Packs

1. What's the Idea?

Design small travel journal kits with prompts, blank pages, and stickers for kids to document trips, vacations, or school field trips.

2. Why It Could Work

Traveling families want ways to keep kids engaged. A kid-designed journal makes it more exciting to capture memories.

3. Who Might Be Your Customer?

- Families planning trips
- Teachers for class field trips
- Gift buyers before summer or holidays

4. Steps to Get Started (and Budget)

Estimated Startup Budget: $10–$30

- Print booklets with prompts like "Today I saw..." or "Favorite food of the trip"

- Include stickers, pens, or small envelopes for keepsakes
- Package as a travel bundle
- Sell for $5–$12 per kit

5. Pro Tips

- Offer different designs (road trip, airplane travel, international)
- Include map coloring pages or language fun facts
- Promote as "Screen-Free Travel Fun"

Tags: Educational, Travel-Based, Moderate Budget

Good for kids who: Love writing, traveling, and creativity

Idea 69: Mini Home Movie Theater Kits

1. What's the Idea?

Put together a kit that includes popcorn, themed tickets, movie night signs, and snack trays for families to host their own "theater night" at home.

2. Why It Could Work

Families love movie night. A ready-to-go kit makes it more fun and special—especially as a gift or weekend treat.

3. Who Might Be Your Customer?

- Families with young kids
- Birthday party hosts
- Gift buyers for holidays

4. Steps to Get Started (and Budget)

Estimated Startup Budget: $20–$50

- Include popcorn bags, snack trays, printable tickets, and signs

- Add glow sticks or drink cups for extra flair
- Offer different kits: "Classic," "Princess," "Superhero," etc.
- Price at $10–$20 per kit

5. Pro Tips

- Include printable "Now Showing" signs
- Create a Spotify playlist with movie music
- Offer refill packs for repeat movie nights

Tags: Event-Based, Family-Friendly, Moderate Budget

Good for kids who: Like planning events, crafting fun kits, and spreading joy

Idea 70: DIY Tie-Dye T-Shirt Business

1. What's the Idea?

Make colorful, one-of-a-kind tie-dye T-shirts and sell them at school, local events, or online (with adult help).

2. Why It Could Work

Tie-dye is always popular, and people love wearing something that feels fun, personal, and handmade.

3. Who Might Be Your Customer?

- Kids and teens
- Parents looking for unique gifts
- Summer camps or sports teams

4. Steps to Get Started (and Budget)

Estimated Startup Budget: $30–$75

- Buy white shirts and a tie-dye kit (or mix your own)
- Create a few designs (spiral, heart, stripes)

- Let them dry fully and package with care
- Price between $10–$20 per shirt
- Offer custom orders (colors, name initials, etc.)

5. Pro Tips

- Bundle with matching scrunchies or socks
- Create themed collections (school spirit, rainbow, neon)
- Wash and dry before selling so they're ready to wear

Tags: Fashion-Based, Creative, Moderate Budget

Good for kids who: Love color, hands-on projects, and wearable art

Idea 71: "Lost & Found" Organizer

1. What's the Idea?

Offer a weekly service to organize, sort, and display items from the school's lost and found to help classmates reclaim their stuff.

2. Why It Could Work

Lost & Found piles are a mess at most schools. Helping clean and organize it is useful, appreciated, and builds responsibility.

3. Who Might Be Your Customer?

- School staff
- PTA or principal
- Classmates and parents

4. Steps to Get Started (and Budget)

Estimated Startup Budget: Free–$10

- Ask permission from school staff to help organize
- Create signs or posters ("Check the Lost & Found Today!")

- Sort by category (jackets, lunch boxes, water bottles)
- Offer a weekly or monthly "display day"
- Optional: create a simple tip jar or reward box

5. Pro Tips

- Take before-and-after photos to show your work
- Offer a donation bag service for unclaimed items
- Be consistent and helpful—it builds trust

Tags: School-Friendly, Helping Hands, Free/Low Budget

Good for kids who: Like organizing, helping others, and improving their school

Idea 72: Ice Cream Topping Stand

1. What's the Idea?

Set up a small stand (with adult help) offering bowls or cones with ice cream toppings only—people bring their own ice cream!

2. Why It Could Work

Topping bars are fun and interactive. You don't need to handle cold ice cream—just the toppings, which makes it easier and cheaper.

3. Who Might Be Your Customer?

- Kids at school events or sports games
- Birthday party hosts
- Summer block parties

4. Steps to Get Started (and Budget)

Estimated Startup Budget: $20–$50

- Buy toppings: sprinkles, chocolate chips, gummy bears, whipped cream

239

- Offer cups with a "build your own" setup
- Keep everything clean and allergy-safe
- Charge $2–$4 per serving or offer family packs
- Use signs and gloves—make it look official!

5. Pro Tips

- Create fun combos like "Unicorn Crunch" or "Choco-Blast"
- Partner with someone selling ice cream or popsicles
- Keep everything cool and safe—no spoilable items

Tags: Food-Based, Event-Friendly, Moderate Budget

Good for kids who: Like serving others, being part of events, and having fun with food

Idea 73: Morning School DJ

1. What's the Idea?

Play fun music for morning arrival at school or during lunch (with permission), creating a good vibe and possibly earning tips or donations.

2. Why It Could Work

Good music makes mornings better. A kid-led DJ booth brings energy and positivity—plus, you get to share your favorite tunes!

3. Who Might Be Your Customer?

- School community
- PTO or student council
- Classmates who love music

4. Steps to Get Started (and Budget)

Estimated Startup Budget: Free–$30

- Ask your school for permission and sound rules
- Use a Bluetooth speaker or small setup

- Curate playlists that are upbeat and appropriate
- Offer special request days or shout-outs
- Optionally collect tips or get small funding from the PTA

5. Pro Tips

- Create theme days: "Throwback Thursday," "Dance Friday"
- Keep volume controlled and respectful
- Be consistent and professional—build your rep!

Tags: Music-Based, School-Friendly, Low Budget

Good for kids who: Love music, curating playlists, and hyping up a crowd

Idea 74: DIY Greeting Card Packs

1. What's the Idea?

Design and sell handmade or digitally created greeting cards in packs—for birthdays, holidays, thank-yous, and more.

2. Why It Could Work

Greeting cards are always in demand. A card made by a kid adds a personal and meaningful touch, especially when bundled into themed packs.

3. Who Might Be Your Customer?

- Parents and grandparents
- Gift shoppers
- Teachers looking for class card sets

4. Steps to Get Started (and Budget)

Estimated Startup Budget: $10–$30

- Make 3–6 designs using markers or digital tools

- Print on cardstock or quality paper
- Bundle 4–10 cards per pack with envelopes
- Sell each pack for $5–$12 depending on quantity and design
- Market as "kid-created" and perfect for gifting

5. Pro Tips

- Offer personalization or blank insides
- Sell seasonal packs: holidays, birthdays, teacher thank-yous
- Add hand-drawn touches or sticker accents for uniqueness

Tags: Creative, Gift-Friendly, Low/Moderate Budget

Good for kids who: Enjoy drawing, card-making, and spreading joy

Idea 75: Kid Recipe Blog or Zine

1. What's the Idea?

Write and publish simple recipes, cooking tips, or snack ideas—either as a blog, printed zine, or downloadable booklet.

2. Why It Could Work

Kids love reading recipes from other kids. A blog or booklet is a fun way to share food knowledge while building writing and design skills.

3. Who Might Be Your Customer?

- Families looking for kid-friendly recipes
- Teachers or homeschool groups
- Aspiring kid chefs

4. Steps to Get Started (and Budget)

Estimated Startup Budget: Free–$30

- Choose 5–10 simple recipes and test them
- Add photos, drawings, and cooking tips

- Publish as a blog, printable PDF, or small printed booklet
- Offer free samples and charge $3–$7 per issue or download
- Share through family, school, or social media (with adult help)

5. Pro Tips

- Include allergy tips or substitutions
- Try themed issues (breakfast, snacks, holiday baking)
- Ask friends for recipes to create a "Kid Chef Collab" edition

Tags: Educational, Digital/Print, Low Budget

Good for kids who: Love cooking, writing, and helping others learn

Idea 76: DIY Locker Mirror Sets

1. What's the Idea?

Decorate and sell mini mirrors with frames, magnets, and positive affirmations—perfect for school lockers.

2. Why It Could Work

Lockers are prime real estate for fun accessories. A locker mirror is both useful and a fun way to express personality.

3. Who Might Be Your Customer?

- Middle school students
- Parents buying back-to-school gifts
- Classmates or teachers for prizes

4. Steps to Get Started (and Budget)

Estimated Startup Budget: $20–$50

- Buy small craft mirrors and attach magnets
- Decorate frames with washi tape, stickers, or quotes

- Package with a gift pouch or note card
- Sell for $4–$10 each depending on style
- Display in bundles or as part of a locker décor kit

5. Pro Tips

- Offer custom name or initial options
- Pair with matching magnets or notes
- Keep packaging compact for school events or locker sales

Tags: School-Friendly, Fashion & Decor, Moderate Budget

Good for kids who: Like crafting, fashion, and school accessories

Idea 77: Puzzle Hunt Creator

1. What's the Idea?

Design puzzle or scavenger hunt experiences—either printable at-home kits or live hunts for birthday parties or classrooms.

2. Why It Could Work

People love solving mysteries and clues. A fun puzzle challenge or treasure hunt can be both entertaining and educational.

3. Who Might Be Your Customer?

- Parents planning parties
- Teachers looking for fun classroom activities
- Kids wanting creative birthday fun

4. Steps to Get Started (and Budget)

Estimated Startup Budget: Free–$20

- Create 5–10 clue cards, riddles, or puzzles
- Format for printing or email delivery

- Sell themed kits: "Spy Mission," "Lost Treasure," "Holiday Heist"
- Price at $5–$12 per kit depending on complexity
- Optionally offer to set up in person (with adult help)

5. Pro Tips

- Add a "Grand Prize" suggestion for parents to hide
- Include difficulty levels (easy/medium/hard)
- Offer custom versions with names or school subjects

Tags: Educational, Event-Friendly, Low Budget

Good for kids who: Love puzzles, storytelling, and game design

Idea 78: Digital Pet Certificates

1. What's the Idea?

Design fun certificates for pets—like "Best Dog Ever," "Cutest Cat in the House," or "Hamster of the Month"—and sell printable or customized versions.

2. Why It Could Work

People love their pets and enjoy showing them off. A fun certificate makes for a great gift or family laugh.

3. Who Might Be Your Customer?

- Pet owners
- Kids who want to reward their pets
- Gift givers

4. Steps to Get Started (and Budget)

Estimated Startup Budget: Free–$10

- Design templates using Canva or similar tools

- Include space for pet name, photo, and award
- Sell as instant downloads or offer custom versions
- Price at $2–$5 for printables, $5–$10 for custom
- Offer bundles (3 awards for $12)

5. Pro Tips

- Add seasonal awards (e.g., "Howl-o-Ween Costume Champ")
- Include matching sticker or badge designs
- Keep fonts and colors playful and pet-friendly

Tags: Pet-Based, Digital Product, Free/Low Budget

Good for kids who: Love animals, design, and making people smile

Idea 79: Personalized Name Pencil Sets

1. What's the Idea?

Create sets of pencils with kids' names, phrases, or custom colors using stickers, engraving tools, or vinyl lettering.

2. Why It Could Work

Kids lose pencils constantly. Having your name on them is practical— and makes supplies feel special and personalized.

3. Who Might Be Your Customer?

- Classmates and friends
- Parents for school supply shopping
- Teachers giving gifts or rewards

4. Steps to Get Started (and Budget)

Estimated Startup Budget: $15–$40

- Buy basic pencils in fun colors
- Use sticker letters, stamps, or a label maker to personalize

- Group 5–10 pencils per set and tie with ribbon or put in a pouch
- Price at $4–$8 per set depending on design
- Take orders through an order form or flyer

5. Pro Tips

- Offer motivational phrases like "Keep Going!" or "Homework Hero"
- Create color themes (neon, galaxy, pastel)
- Sell bundles with matching erasers or notebooks

Tags: School-Friendly, Customizable, Low/Moderate Budget

Good for kids who: Enjoy personalization, school supplies, and gift giving

Idea 80: TikTok Trends Reporter

1. What's the Idea?

Write a short weekly newsletter or blog sharing fun and safe TikTok trends, challenges, and sounds for other kids and parents to enjoy or stay updated. Really the newsletter can be on any topic that you are interested. Not just TikTok trends. There are endless interesting niche topics that you could create a weekly update or report most likely in the form of a newsletter or maybe TikTok or Instagram channel.

2. Why It Could Work

Not everyone has TikTok—or the time to scroll forever. A trend roundup from a fellow kid is helpful and fun to read.

3. Who Might Be Your Customer?

- Kids who aren't allowed on TikTok
- Parents trying to stay in the loop
- Teachers or youth leaders

4. Steps to Get Started (and Budget)

Estimated Startup Budget: Free–$10

- Research and write about 3–5 fun trends each week
- Include screenshots, tips, or "how-to" instructions
- Share via email (with parent help) or create a print version
- Offer free previews and charge $1–$2/month for full access

5. Pro Tips

- Keep everything age-appropriate and positive
- Offer a "Top 5 Sounds" list each week
- Include "Parent Tips" or "Safe Apps" section

Tags: Digital Product, Trend-Based, Free/Low Budget

Good for kids who: Love pop culture, writing, and discovering new trends

Idea 81: Origami Surprise Packs

1. What's the Idea?

Fold and sell mystery packs of origami creations—each pack contains animals, notes, or mini challenges.

2. Why It Could Work

Origami is cool, calming, and collectible. Surprise packs add excitement and are perfect for party favors or classroom fun.

3. Who Might Be Your Customer?

- Students and friends
- Birthday party shoppers
- Teachers giving classroom prizes

4. Steps to Get Started (and Budget)

Estimated Startup Budget: Under $15

- Fold animals, shapes, hearts, fortune tellers, etc.
- Package 3–5 items per envelope with a label

- Add a mystery challenge ("Make your own crane!")
- Price at $2–$4 per pack
- Sell at school or bundle as gift sets

5. Pro Tips

- Use colorful patterned paper or seasonal colors
- Include a folded note with a fun fact or positive message
- Offer custom birthday or holiday-themed versions

Tags: Creative, Collectible, Low Budget

Good for kids who: Love origami, surprises, and folding crafts

Idea 82: Sidewalk Chalk Artist for Hire

1. What's the Idea?

Offer to create sidewalk chalk art for birthdays, welcome signs, or inspirational quotes in front of homes or businesses.

2. Why It Could Work

Chalk art is eye-catching and cheerful. It's also temporary—so it's a great way to mark a special occasion without a big setup.

3. Who Might Be Your Customer?

- Parents throwing birthday parties
- Neighbors celebrating milestones
- Local businesses wanting cheerful messages

4. Steps to Get Started (and Budget)

Estimated Startup Budget: $10–$30

- Buy good-quality chalk and a kneeling pad
- Offer different packages: "Happy Birthday," "Congrats," "Wel-

come Home"
- Create a flyer or post on neighborhood groups (with adult help)
- Charge $5–$15 per design depending on size/detail

5. Pro Tips

- Sketch the layout on paper first
- Offer themed options (unicorns, dinosaurs, sports)
- Take photos to build a portfolio of your work

Tags: Creative, Event-Friendly, Low Budget

Good for kids who: Love art, celebrations, and working outdoors

Idea 83: Snack Reviewer Channel or Blog

1. What's the Idea?

Start a fun blog, YouTube channel, or social post series where you review snacks—local, international, weird combos, or DIY creations. Earn ad revenue and other sponsorship deals as follower count grows.

2. Why It Could Work

Everyone eats snacks. A funny, honest kid review helps people discover new ones—and can be entertaining and educational.

3. Who Might Be Your Customer?

- Friends and classmates
- Parents looking for new lunchbox ideas
- Snack lovers of all ages

4. Steps to Get Started (and Budget)

Estimated Startup Budget: $10–$30

- Buy a few snacks to review each week

- Rate them on taste, texture, packaging, and fun
- Create short written reviews, videos, or TikToks
- Promote with a consistent name and schedule
- Offer bonus content (e.g., Top 10 of the Month)

5. Pro Tips

- Keep reviews short, funny, and honest
- Ask friends to guest-star in episodes
- Follow safety rules with all food content

Tags: Digital Content, Food-Based, Low/Moderate Budget

Good for kids who: Love snacks, talking on camera, and sharing opinions

Idea 84: Kid Photographer for Events & Local Businesses

1. What's the Idea?

Offer photography services for birthday parties, school events, sports games—or take product and lifestyle photos for local businesses that want better images for their website or social media.

2. Why It Could Work

Everyone needs good photos. Families want to remember special moments, and small businesses need better pictures of their products or services—but they don't always want to hire expensive professionals. That's where you come in!

3. Who Might Be Your Customer?

- Parents hosting events or parties
- Coaches or teams wanting game photos
- Local businesses (bakeries, salons, boutiques, restaurants)
- Classmates or friends needing portraits or pet photos

4. Steps to Get Started (and Budget)

Estimated Startup Budget: Free–$50

- Practice taking photos of people, pets, products, or food
- Build a small portfolio using photos of your own items or friends' businesses
- Offer a free trial shoot to one local business or family
- Create a flyer or simple website to promote your services
- Charge $15–$75 per shoot depending on length and type

5. Pro Tips

- Learn basic photo editing with free apps like Snapseed or Canva
- Bring a list of shots to capture (e.g., wide, close-up, behind-the-scenes)
- Offer digital files, printed photos, or social media-ready images
- Always ask for permission and be professional—your reputation matters!

Tags: Creative, Service-Based, Moderate Budget

Good for kids who: Love photography, enjoy working with people, and want to support their local community

Idea 85: YouTube Thumbnail Designer

1. What's the Idea?

Design eye-catching thumbnails for YouTubers who need help making their videos stand out with great titles and visuals.

2. Why It Could Work

A good thumbnail can make or break a video. Many beginner YouTubers don't know how to design them or want to save time.

3. Who Might Be Your Customer?

- Kids who have YouTube or gaming channels
- Tweens or teens who stream or post content
- Family vloggers or student creators

4. Steps to Get Started (and Budget)

Estimated Startup Budget: Free–$15

- Learn Canva, Photopea, or other free tools
- Create 5–10 sample thumbnails in different styles

- Offer $3–$7 per thumbnail or bundle prices
- Take orders through Google Forms or a simple website

5. Pro Tips

- Include a few free "starter templates"
- Study top YouTubers to learn what works
- Offer different fonts, color palettes, and layout choices

Tags: Tech-Friendly, Digital Design, Free/Low Budget

Good for kids who: Like graphic design, YouTube, and creating bold visuals

Idea 86: Balloon Art & Decorations

1. What's the Idea?

Create colorful balloon garlands or arches for parties, school dances, or local businesses using pre-inflated or DIY kits.

2. Why It Could Work

Balloon displays are trending at parties and events. If you can make them look awesome, people will gladly pay for your help.

3. Who Might Be Your Customer?

- Parents planning birthdays
- School dance committees
- Businesses doing pop-up events or store openings

4. Steps to Get Started (and Budget)

Estimated Startup Budget: $40–$75

- Watch YouTube tutorials on making balloon garlands
- Buy balloon kits, strips, and hand/foot pumps

- Offer setup services or sell pre-bundled DIY kits
- Charge $20–$50 depending on size and materials

5. Pro Tips

- Offer color themes (pastel, neon, rainbow, school spirit)
- Add bonus items like confetti or hanging streamers
- Take photos of each setup for your portfolio

Tags: Event-Based, Visual Design, Moderate Budget

Good for kids who: Enjoy decorating, parties, and hands-on projects

Idea 87: Personalized Digital Certificates for Kids

1. What's the Idea?

Design and sell digital certificates for accomplishments like "Great Reader," "Homework Hero," or "Super Friend Award."

2. Why It Could Work

Kids love being recognized. Parents and teachers love giving out fun, personalized awards that motivate and boost confidence.

3. Who Might Be Your Customer?

- Teachers and tutors
- Parents of younger kids
- Homeschooling families

4. Steps to Get Started (and Budget)

Estimated Startup Budget: Free–$10

- Create certificate templates in Canva or Google Slides

- Offer editable PDFs or custom-made versions
- Price at $2–$5 per digital certificate
- Bundle packs for teachers (5 or 10-pack options)

5. Pro Tips

- Include seasonal awards (e.g., "Fall Reading Champion")
- Offer colorful, black-and-white, or printable formats
- Add a space for the child's name, date, and signature line

Tags: Educational, Digital Product, Low Budget

Good for kids who: Like design, motivation, and helping others feel special

Idea 88: Gift Wrapping Service

1. What's the Idea?

Offer to wrap small gifts for holidays, birthdays, or events using fun paper, tags, and bows—especially around busy seasons.

2. Why It Could Work

Gift-wrapping takes time, and not everyone's good at it! A kid offering this service is helpful and can make presents look awesome.

3. Who Might Be Your Customer?

- Neighbors or friends during holidays
- Parents needing help before events
- Teachers or school fundraisers

4. Steps to Get Started (and Budget)

Estimated Startup Budget: $10–$30

- Collect wrapping supplies (paper, tape, ribbon, tags)
- Offer flat-rate pricing (e.g., $1–$3 per gift depending on size)

- Advertise with flyers or word-of-mouth
- Set up at school or host "Wrap It Day" with parent help

5. Pro Tips

- Offer themes (birthday, holiday, sports, animals)
- Add handmade tags or optional messages
- Keep gift sizes small and manageable

Tags: Service-Based, Seasonal, Low Budget

Good for kids who: Like wrapping, decorating, and helping others prepare

Idea 89: DIY Fortune Cookie Packs

1. What's the Idea?

Make and sell your own fortune cookies—with custom kid-written fortunes inside—or offer "Fortune Kits" for others to bake their own.

2. Why It Could Work

They're fun to eat and even more fun to read! Fortune cookies are great for birthdays, parties, and little surprises.

3. Who Might Be Your Customer?

- Party hosts
- Parents giving creative gifts
- Teachers using them in class

4. Steps to Get Started (and Budget)

Estimated Startup Budget: $15–$40

- Bake cookies using a basic fortune cookie recipe
- Write creative or funny fortunes ahead of time

- Package in small bundles (3–6 cookies) with a label
- Sell for $4–$10 per pack

5. Pro Tips

- Offer themed fortunes: birthday, school success, silly jokes
- Include a blank version for people to write their own
- Be sure to label for allergies and use adult supervision

Tags: Food-Based, Creative, Moderate Budget

Good for kids who: Love baking, writing, and fun surprises

Idea 90: Birthday Countdown Calendars

1. What's the Idea?

Create mini countdown calendars that help kids count down the days to their birthday—with jokes, challenges, or small surprises on each day.

2. Why It Could Work

Kids love the excitement of counting down to big events. A birthday countdown makes the celebration feel longer and more fun!

3. Who Might Be Your Customer?

- Parents planning birthdays
- Kids giving gifts to friends
- Teachers for student birthday rewards

4. Steps to Get Started (and Budget)

Estimated Startup Budget: $10−$25

- Design a 5- to 10-day countdown calendar

- Add jokes, kind challenges, or little prize ideas under each flap
- Package with markers or stickers
- Price at $5–$10 per calendar

5. Pro Tips

- Offer custom versions with names or themes
- Include optional "coupon" surprises for small favors
- Make a printable version for digital buyers

Tags: Event-Based, Giftable, Low/Moderate Budget

Good for kids who: Like celebrating, making people smile, and designing creative gifts

Idea 91: YouTube Channel Intro Maker

1. What's the Idea?

Design short animated or text-based intro videos for YouTube creators to place at the beginning of their videos.

2. Why It Could Work

Everyone wants a cool intro to make their videos look more professional. If you can create fun animations, this is a great niche.

3. Who Might Be Your Customer?

- Beginner YouTubers
- Friends who stream content
- Kids launching a school project or vlog

4. Steps to Get Started (and Budget)

Estimated Startup Budget: Free–$20

- Learn to use tools like Canva, CapCut, or Adobe Spark
- Offer templates with name, slogan, and theme music

- Deliver video file (.mp4) and offer edits
- Charge $5–$15 per intro, or bundles with outros too

5. Pro Tips

- Create 3–5 demo styles to show your work
- Offer matching thumbnails or banners
- Keep music copyright-safe using royalty-free sites

Tags: Digital Product, Tech & Video, Low Budget

Good for kids who: Enjoy animation, editing, and helping creators stand out

Idea 92: Classroom Job Chart Designer

1. What's the Idea?

Design and sell custom job charts for teachers to use in class, helping them assign and rotate classroom responsibilities.

2. Why It Could Work

Teachers appreciate ready-made tools that are cute and functional. A student-made chart is even more relatable!

3. Who Might Be Your Customer?

- Elementary school teachers
- Homeschool parents
- Tutors or daycare providers

4. Steps to Get Started (and Budget)

Estimated Startup Budget: Free–$15

- Create fun, easy-to-read chart templates (digital or printable)
- Include job titles like "Line Leader" or "Tech Helper"

- Offer editable versions or printed laminated sets
- Price at $4–$10 depending on version

5. Pro Tips

- Add matching name tags or reward trackers
- Offer holiday or themed sets
- Ask a teacher for feedback before launching

Tags: Educational, School-Based, Low Budget

Good for kids who: Enjoy classroom life, design, and helping others stay organized

Idea 93: "Homework Hero" Starter Packs

1. What's the Idea?

Create motivational homework kits with pencils, notepads, stickers, and encouraging messages to help kids tackle their schoolwork.

2. Why It Could Work

Homework can feel like a drag—but a fun kit with the right tools (and attitude) can make it feel like a mission worth completing.

3. Who Might Be Your Customer?

- Parents helping kids stay focused
- Teachers rewarding effort
- Gift buyers looking for school-themed bundles

4. Steps to Get Started (and Budget)

Estimated Startup Budget: $20–$40

- Gather fun supplies (cute pencils, notebooks, sticky notes)
- Add printed encouragement cards or "Homework Hero" badges

- Package in pencil cases or drawstring bags
- Sell each kit for $7–$15

5. Pro Tips

- Offer themed kits: math, reading, science
- Include a "goal tracker" or reward chart
- Create refill packs for returning customers

Tags: Educational, Giftable, Moderate Budget

Good for kids who: Like organizing, school supplies, and encouraging others

Idea 94: Virtual Background Sticker Packs

1. What's the Idea?

Design and sell themed sticker overlays (transparent PNGs) that kids can use on Zoom backgrounds or during virtual presentations.

2. Why It Could Work

Virtual life isn't going away anytime soon. Kids love personalizing their screens with fun graphics—especially during school or video calls.

3. Who Might Be Your Customer?

- Students attending virtual classes
- Teachers adding fun to remote lessons
- Kids in virtual clubs or hobby groups

4. Steps to Get Started (and Budget)

Estimated Startup Budget: Free–$10

- Design PNG sticker sets (headbands, sunglasses, animals, etc.)

- Bundle 10–20 images per theme pack
- Deliver as a ZIP file or Google Drive link
- Price at $3–$6 per pack

5. Pro Tips

- Include instructions for using stickers in Zoom or Canva
- Offer seasonal packs (Halloween, Winter, School Spirit)
- Add a bonus "Create Your Own Sticker" page

Tags: Digital Product, Tech & Fun, Low Budget

Good for kids who: Love virtual tools, graphic design, and creative expression

Idea 95: Business Idea Coach for Other Kids

1. What's the Idea?

Use everything you've learned to help other kids brainstorm, plan, or launch their own small businesses—offering advice, idea sessions, or startup support.

2. Why It Could Work

Once you've started your own business (even a small one), you've learned lessons others haven't. Helping someone else get started can be both inspiring and profitable!

3. Who Might Be Your Customer?

- Friends or classmates who want to start something
- Younger kids looking for ideas
- Parents or teachers looking for guidance for their students

4. Steps to Get Started (and Budget)

Estimated Startup Budget: Free–$10

- Make a flyer or website offering "Kid Business Coaching"
- Create a list of your business experiences and tips
- Offer 15–30 min idea sessions (in person or via Zoom)
- Charge a flat fee ($5–$15) or offer it for free to get testimonials
- Optionally include a printable workbook or brainstorming sheet

5. Pro Tips

- Help with things like naming a business, goal setting, or first steps
- Make it fun and supportive—not too serious!
- Celebrate the launch of every business you help start

Tags: Leadership, Educational, Free/Low Budget

Good for kids who: Love helping others, speaking confidently, and sharing what they've learned

Idea 96: Neighborhood Helper Bundle

1. What's the Idea?

Offer a weekly service bundle for neighbors that includes taking out garbage/recycling bins, bringing in mail or packages, and doing quick porch or front yard checks while they're busy or out of town.

2. Why It Could Work

People want peace of mind when they're away—or just help managing little tasks each week. Bundling simple services saves them time, and earns you steady, reliable income.

3. Who Might Be Your Customer?

- Elderly neighbors
- Families who travel often
- Busy professionals
- Snowbirds or weekend homeowners

4. Steps to Get Started (and Budget)

Estimated Startup Budget: Free

- Make a flyer offering your "Weekly Helper Service"
- Offer tiered pricing depending on what they need
- Basic: Trash/recycling bin help ($1–$2/week)
- Standard: Add mail/package pickup (+$1/week)
- Premium: Add vacation house check-ins (+$2/week)
- Set up a simple schedule and keep track in a notebook or phone
- Collect payments weekly or monthly

5. Pro Tips

- Be extremely reliable—this is about trust
- Take photos or text quick updates for out-of-town customers
- Offer one-time or short-term coverage during vacations
- Include extras like watering plants or sweeping the porch for a small upcharge

Tags: Service-Based, Neighborhood, Free Budget

Good for kids who: Are organized, trustworthy, and want steady weekly income from simple, helpful tasks

Idea 97: Lemonade Stand (with a Twist!)

1. What's the Idea?

Set up a lemonade stand in a busy location—or take it further by creating your own lemonade *brand* with unique flavors, packaging, and signs that make people stop and say, "I want that."

2. Why It Could Work

A lemonade stand is one of the most classic kid businesses ever—and it still works! With the right location (think parks, sports games, busy corners), a well-run stand can bring in **$50–$100+ per hour**. And if you treat it like a real brand? Even better.

3. Who Might Be Your Customer?

- Thirsty neighbors or park-goers
- Parents and kids at sports fields
- Walkers, bikers, and anyone outside on a hot day

4. Steps to Get Started (and Budget)

Estimated Startup Budget: $10–$40

- Pick your lemonade style: classic, pink, or custom flavors (lavender, mint, berry)
- Use powdered mix, fresh lemons, or a family recipe
- Decorate your stand with signs, pricing, and your **brand name**
- Offer small, medium, and large sizes (or create fun combos!)
- Set up in a high-traffic, **safe and approved** location with adult supervision
- Sell for $1–$3 per cup depending on quality and area

5. Pro Tips

- Brand it! Come up with a business name like "Fresh Squeeze Co." or "Sunshine Lemonade"
- Offer upsells: lemon cookies, bracelets, or stickers
- Create loyalty cards ("Buy 5, get 1 free!")
- Wear matching shirts or aprons to look official
- Add a tip jar—people often tip if you're friendly and enthusiastic!

Tags: Classic, Food-Based, Creative, Moderate Budget

Good for kids who: Like face-to-face selling, branding, and creating fun experiences

Idea 98: Lawn Mowing & Seasonal Yard Services

1. What's the Idea?

Start a lawn mowing business that also offers simple property upkeep like leaf raking, weeding, and—when the weather changes—snow shoveling in the winter. You can even give your business a name and offer year-round service plans.

2. Why It Could Work

Yard work never ends. In spring and summer, people need their lawns mowed. In fall, leaves pile up. In winter, driveways and sidewalks need shoveling. Many families would gladly pay a responsible kid to take care of these regular chores.

3. Who Might Be Your Customer?

- Neighbors with yards or long driveways
- Elderly homeowners
- Busy families or traveling homeowners
- Local landlords or Airbnb hosts

4. Steps to Get Started (and Budget)

Estimated Startup Budget: $0–$100 (depending on tools)

- Use your own mower or borrow one from family
- Create a flyer with pricing for:
- Lawn mowing ($15–$40 depending on size)
- Leaf raking or garden bed cleanup ($10–$30 per job)
- Snow shoveling ($15–$50 depending on driveway size)
- Offer weekly, bi-weekly, or one-time services
- Ask satisfied customers for referrals or offer a "neighbor discount"

5. Pro Tips

- Brand your service: name it something like "Next Gen Yard Care" or "Fresh Cut & Clear"
- Bundle services: e.g., Lawn + Leaf Cleanup = Save $5
- Create seasonal postcards to hand out each quarter (spring = mowing, fall = leaves, winter = snow, etc.)
- Keep a checklist of each job so you stay consistent
- Be dependable—people love hiring someone they can count on

Tags: Service-Based, Seasonal, Outdoor Work

Good for kids who: Are strong, dependable, and want to earn steady money helping neighbors

Idea 99: Neighborhood Car Wash Service

1. What's the Idea?

Offer car washing services right in your neighbors' driveways. Bring your own supplies or use theirs (with permission), and leave each car sparkling clean—inside, outside, or both!

2. Why It Could Work

Lots of people want a clean car but don't have the time to do it themselves—and don't want to drive to a car wash. A friendly, local kid who shows up on time and does a great job? That's an easy yes.

3. Who Might Be Your Customer?

- Neighbors with multiple cars
- Parents with messy backseats
- Elderly residents or people who don't want to drive to a car wash
- Anyone prepping for a road trip or special event

4. Steps to Get Started (and Budget)
   Estimated Startup Budget: $10–$30

- Gather supplies: bucket, sponges, car soap, microfiber towels, vacuum (optional)
- Offer packages like:
- **Basic Exterior Wash** ($10–$15)
- **Exterior + Interior Vacuum** ($50–$100)
- **Full Detail** with windows and dashboard wiped down ($100–$200+)
- Go door-to-door or leave flyers on mailboxes
- Ask if you can use their hose and driveway, or offer to bring a water jug

5. Pro Tips

- Use a checklist to make sure nothing gets missed
- Offer weekly or bi-weekly "Car Care Plans" for repeat business
- Use tire shine, air fresheners, or dashboard polish to stand out
- Keep towels clean and rotate often—quality matters
- Create a loyalty card (buy 5 washes, get 1 free)

Tags: Service-Based, Neighborhood-Friendly, Low Budget

Good for kids who: Are detail-oriented, enjoy physical work, and want to build a loyal customer base

Idea 100: Window Washing Business

1. What's the Idea?

Start a simple window cleaning service for homes or small businesses. Offer to clean exterior (and possibly interior) windows, making them shine like new.

2. Why It Could Work

Clean windows make a house or storefront look better, but a lot of people don't want to do it themselves—especially on the outside or on higher windows. A responsible kid offering this service for an affordable price can easily stand out.

3. Who Might Be Your Customer?

- Homeowners (especially elderly or busy families)
- Storefront businesses with lots of windows
- Realtors preparing houses for sale
- Airbnb or vacation rental hosts

4. Steps to Get Started (and Budget)

Estimated Startup Budget: $20–$100

- Get basic supplies: squeegee, bucket, sponge, vinegar or window cleaner, microfiber cloths
- Offer service packages:
- **Small Job (5–10 windows):** $10–$30
- **Full House (10–25 windows):** $30–$100+
- Ask customers to remove window screens beforehand (or do it for them with permission)
- Hand out flyers or post in a neighborhood group
- Bring a small step stool or ladder (with adult supervision if needed)

5. Pro Tips

- Use a squeegee and dry towel for streak-free results
- Offer a rain-check guarantee (if it rains within 24 hours, come back and rewipe!)
- Bundle with other services like mailbox cleaning, porch sweeping, or trash bin help
- Take before-and-after photos to show your work and build trust

Tags: Service-Based, Home Care, Low Budget

Good for kids who: Like outdoor work, attention to detail, and helping homes shine

Idea 101: Sports Card Trading & Sales Business

1. What's the Idea?

Buy, sell, and trade sports cards (like baseball, basketball, or Pokémon-style sports inserts) online or in-person. You can flip cards for profit, run a table at a local show, or even start a mini card club with friends.

2. Why It Could Work

Sports card collecting is back in a big way. Some cards are worth pennies, others are worth hundreds—or even thousands. If you learn how to spot value, stay up to date on hot players, and treat it like a real business, you can build something exciting and profitable.

3. Who Might Be Your Customer?

- Other kids or collectors at school
- Hobby shops or collectors at local card shows
- Buyers on platforms like eBay, Mercari, or Whatnot (with parent help)

4. Steps to Get Started (and Budget)

Estimated Startup Budget: $20–$100+ (depending on your collection or initial packs)

- Start with cards you already own or buy starter packs/boxes
- Learn how to check card values using eBay "sold" listings or apps like CollX or Card Ladder
- Sell individual cards in-person, online, or trade up to better ones
- Keep cards in great condition—use sleeves, top-loaders, and binders
- Take clear photos and write honest descriptions if selling online

5. Pro Tips

- Focus on rising stars or hot rookies in sports (value can increase quickly)
- Offer "Mystery Packs" with 5–10 random cards for a flat price
- Trade smart—don't give away high-value cards without doing your homework
- Build a reputation as honest and fair—it'll get you repeat buyers
- Consider creating your own mini sports card club at school or in your neighborhood

Tags: Collectibles, Buy/Sell/Trade, Hobby-Based

Good for kids who: Love sports, enjoy collecting, and want to turn a hobby into a real business

Idea 102: Home Gardening Helper

1. What's the Idea?

Offer regular help with home gardens—watering plants, applying fertilizer, pulling weeds, and keeping things looking healthy and tidy. Think of it as being a mini plant care consultant or assistant for busy homeowners.

2. Why It Could Work

Many people love having a garden, but they're either too busy, forgetful, or physically unable to keep up with the care. A reliable helper who knows how to water, fertilize, and tidy up can be a lifesaver—especially during hot seasons.

3. Who Might Be Your Customer?

- Elderly neighbors or people with limited mobility
- Busy homeowners who travel or work long hours
- Airbnb hosts or vacation homes
- Gardeners who just want extra help

4. Steps to Get Started (and Budget)

Estimated Startup Budget: Free–$20

- Learn basic garden care (watering, weeding, how and when to fertilize)
- Offer a flyer or sign-up sheet with weekly or bi-weekly service options
- Start with basic services:
- Watering plants and garden beds
- Light weeding and deadheading
- Applying fertilizer (with adult guidance or product instructions)
- Charge $5–$15 per visit, depending on size of garden and task list

5. Pro Tips

- Bring your own gloves, watering can, and a small trowel
- Offer seasonal add-ons like planting flowers in spring or mulching in fall
- Create a "Garden Log" for each client to track what you did and when
- Be extra careful with plant types—some require special care
- Ask for a walk-through on the first visit so you know where everything is

Tags: Outdoor, Helping Hands, Eco-Friendly

Good for kids who: Enjoy plants, being outside, and helping things grow

Idea 103: Launch Your Own Product Brand Online

1. What's the Idea?

Find a real product to sell online—on Amazon, Walmart, Etsy, or your own website. You'll source the product (possibly from a factory using Alibaba), create your own brand name, and launch it just like the pros do!

2. Why It Could Work

This is how many real businesses are built today. By finding a product people already want—and making it better, cooler, or more fun—you can build your own brand and sell online to customers all over the world.

3. Who Might Be Your Customer?

- Shoppers on Amazon, Walmart Marketplace, Etsy, or your own site
- Friends, family, and social media followers
- Niche audiences (like gardeners, students, pet owners, athletes, etc.)

4. Steps to Get Started (and Budget)

Estimated Startup Budget: $100–$500+ (depending on product and scale)

- Brainstorm problems to solve or items people buy often (e.g., pencil cases, pet toys, planners, stickers, mini tools)
- Search on **Alibaba.com** or similar platforms for factories that make these products
- Order a few **samples** to check quality (get help from an adult)
- Come up with a **brand name**, logo, and simple packaging
- List your product on Amazon (with help from a parent's seller account), Walmart Marketplace, Etsy, or Shopify
- Promote your product using reviews, photos, and a simple website or social post

5. Pro Tips

- Look for ways to improve a product—cool colors, better packaging, fun extras
- Make sure you **don't copy someone else's trademarked brand or design**
- Read reviews of similar products to see what people love or hate
- Keep your first product **simple** and **lightweight** to reduce shipping costs
- Use free tools like Canva for branding and Fiverr or Upwork for affordable design help

Tags: Product-Based, Branding, eCommerce

Good for kids who: Are creative, like business strategy, and want to launch something real

Idea 104: Kid Book Author & Story Channel Creator

1. What's the Idea?

Write and publish your own children's books—and build a brand around your stories by creating a channel with videos, read-alouds, character updates, or behind-the-scenes content.

2. Why It Could Work

Kids love reading books by other kids! And when you add a YouTube or TikTok channel, website, or podcast to go along with your stories, you're not just selling a book—you're building a **story brand** that grows with your audience.

3. Who Might Be Your Customer?

- Parents looking for books written by kids
- Teachers and librarians wanting fresh, fun reads
- Kids who love original stories, characters, or series
- Fans who discover you through your channel or social media

4. Steps to Get Started (and Budget)

Estimated Startup Budget: $0–$100+ (depending on publishing route)

- Write your first story or book (even short ones work!)
- Use platforms like **Amazon KDP**, **Lulu**, or **Blurb** to self-publish
- Create a simple website or social media account to share your book
- Launch a **YouTube or TikTok channel** where you:
- Read your stories out loud
- Talk about how you created your characters
- Share drawing tutorials or story prompts
- Sell print or digital versions, offer merch (bookmarks, stickers), or bundle books into a series

5. Pro Tips

- Create a consistent brand: same fonts, colors, and character styles
- Ask teachers or librarians if you can do a classroom reading or book signing
- Turn fans into superfans by offering sneak peeks, naming contests, or "fan art" shout-outs
- Repurpose content: your videos can become blog posts, and your stories can become audiobooks!
- Keep improving with each book—writing is like a muscle!

Tags: Creative, Publishing, Content Creation

Good for kids who: Love writing, enjoy storytelling, and want to build a brand around their imagination

Idea 105: Kid Organizer & Declutter Coach

1. What's the Idea?

Offer to help other kids—or even adults—get organized! You can assist with cleaning out messy desks, organizing backpacks or lockers, or even tidying toy bins, art supplies, closets, or drawers.

2. Why It Could Work

Lots of kids (and grownups!) struggle with clutter. A helpful, nonjudgmental kid who offers creative, simple organizing systems can make a big impact—and people will gladly pay for that help.

3. Who Might Be Your Customer?

- Classmates with messy backpacks or lockers
- Parents who need help organizing toy rooms or pantries
- Teachers who want help organizing a classroom supply closet
- Friends or siblings who want to tidy their rooms

4. Steps to Get Started (and Budget)

Estimated Startup Budget: Free–$15

- Offer 30–60 minute organizing sessions for a flat fee ($5–$15)
- Bring labels, markers, and storage bins (or use what's available at the home)
- Create a list of organizing services to offer: toy bins, craft drawers, book shelves, homework stations, etc.
- Take before-and-after photos (with permission) to show your work
- Create a flyer or post that says: "Need help organizing? I've got a system!"

5. Pro Tips

- Start with one area (like school backpacks or desks) to build confidence
- Offer follow-up visits or weekly "reset" sessions for repeat income
- Use fun, colorful labels and keep your organizing kid-friendly
- Suggest mini rewards or games to keep young customers engaged while organizing
- Brand your service: "Tidy by Taylor" or "Organized by Oliver"

Tags: Service-Based, Home & School, Free/Low Budget

Good for kids who: Love organizing, tidying up, and helping others feel more in control

Idea 106: Porch & Entryway & Lawn Decorating Service

1. What's the Idea?

Offer to decorate people's front porches or entryways and/or lawns for holidays, birthdays, or seasons—using signs, flowers, balloons, lights, or themed props to make their home feel festive and welcoming.

2. Why It Could Work

People love cute, seasonal decorations—but many don't have the time or ideas to make it happen. A creative kid offering affordable, low-stress help can make a big impact (and earn repeat customers every season).

3. Who Might Be Your Customer?

- Busy families or elderly neighbors
- Airbnb or vacation rental owners
- Realtors staging homes for sale
- Holiday lovers who just want help

4. Steps to Get Started (and Budget)

Estimated Startup Budget: $100–$200

- Pick a few themes to start: fall, spring, birthdays, 4th of July, Halloween, Christmas holiday etc.
- Offer a flat fee for design and setup ($10–$25) depending on materials
- Use decorations you already own or ask if the customer provides them
- Promote by handing out flyers or posting before/after pics (with permission)
- Offer seasonal subscriptions ("Decorate My Porch Every Month!")

5. Pro Tips

- Keep decorations safe and weather-friendly (no paper in the rain!)
- Offer reusable chalkboard signs, DIY balloon arches, or planter upgrades
- Leave everything neat and clean—first impressions matter
- Bundle with other services like plant watering, mailbox cleanup, or dog walking

Tags: Creative, Service-Based, Seasonal

Good for kids who: Love decorating, working with themes, and helping homes look great

Idea 107: Custom T-Shirt & Merch Designer

1. What's the Idea?

Design your own t-shirts, hoodies, tote bags, or stickers using your original artwork, sayings, or school spirit themes—and sell them online or at local events.

2. Why It Could Work

People love unique designs, especially from young creatives. Whether it's funny slogans, cool art, or trendy school-themed merch, custom gear is always in demand. And now there are tons of easy ways to sell without holding inventory!

3. Who Might Be Your Customer?

- Friends or classmates
- Parents and family
- Local school clubs, teams, or fundraisers
- Online shoppers who love original art

4. Steps to Get Started (and Budget)

Estimated Startup Budget: $0–$50 (can start free with print-on-demand)

- Create designs using Canva, Procreate, or hand drawings
- Use print-on-demand services like **TeeSpring**, **Redbubble**, or **Printful**
- List your items for sale on Etsy, your own website, or via social media
- Promote to friends, family, or during school events
- Offer themed collections (funny quotes, sports, causes, holidays)

5. Pro Tips

- Start with just 1–2 strong designs before creating a full "line"
- Make mockups (images showing your design on real shirts) to attract buyers
- Offer personalization (e.g., name or number on the back) for added value
- Use school colors or neighborhood pride for local appeal
- Host "pre-order" days to avoid buying inventory upfront

Tags: Creative, Product-Based, eCommerce

Good for kids who: Love art, fashion, branding, or starting a real online shop

Idea 108: Custom Keychains

1. What's the Idea?

Create custom keychains using beads, shrink plastic, or resin and sell them at school, events, or online.

2. Why It Could Work

Keychains are small, collectible, and perfect for backpacks or gift bags. You can theme them around school spirit, initials, or favorite hobbies.

3. Who Might Be Your Customer?

- Classmates
- Teachers or parents buying gifts
- People at craft fairs or school events

4. Steps to Get Started (and Budget)

Estimated Startup Budget: $10–$30

- Decide your method: shrink plastic, beaded string, or resin molds
- Create 10–15 samples with different themes

- Package on cardboard backing or in small bags
- Price between $3–$8 depending on style
- Sell in person or with parent help online

5. Pro Tips

- Offer name or letter personalization
- Make matching sets (e.g., best friends or school teams)
- Use fun charms like animals, hearts, or sports gear

Tags: Creative, Fashion-Friendly, Low/Moderate Budget

Good for kids who: Like small crafts, jewelry, or making fun accessories

End Chapter: Now It's Your Turn

First of all—**congratulations.**

You've made it all the way through this book, explored dozens of business ideas, learned practical tools, and gained something most people never do: a head start.

Seriously, just finishing this book puts you ahead of the majority of people who *say* they want to start a business but never actually do. And the best part? You're not just dreaming anymore. You're ready to try.

But before you dive in, let's talk about something that will make a big difference...

🔍 Start by Validating Your Idea

You don't need to launch a full business tomorrow.

First, talk to people.

This step is called **validating demand**—and it's one of the smartest things any entrepreneur (even adults!) can do.

Ask a few potential customers questions like:

- "Would you ever buy something like this?"
- "What would you change about it?"
- "What do you normally do when you need [this problem solved]?"

Listen closely. Not just to compliments—but to **what they really think.**

If someone shrugs and says, "That's cool," that's not enough. You're looking for people who say:

"How soon can I get it?" or

"Can I order one now?"

If no one is interested, that's okay! You just saved time and money. And if people *are* interested? Great—you're onto something.

💡 Build the Simplest Version Possible

You don't need to build a giant business all at once.

Just start with what's called a **Minimum Viable Product** (or MVP). That means:

- Don't buy 1,000 stickers—just print 10.
- Don't try to launch a full slime empire—just sell a few sample kits.
- Don't build a huge website—just make a flyer or a Google Form.

Your first version should be as **small**, **simple**, and **affordable** as possible.

Why? Because it's just a test.

You're testing:

- Will people actually pay for this?
- Is it clear what I'm offering?
- Can I deliver something people truly enjoy?

Once your MVP works, you can improve it and grow. But if it doesn't? You'll know what to fix without wasting tons of time or money.

🌱 Don't Be Afraid to Start Super Small

Every big company you've ever heard of started small:

- Amazon began by selling just **books**—from a garage.
- Nike started by selling shoes **out of the trunk of a car**.
- YouTube was originally a **dating video site** that totally flopped— then pivoted.

You don't need fancy tools, expensive gear, or a team.

You need **a real problem to solve** and a few people who are willing to try what you made.

Starting small isn't just okay—it's smart.

Try This Simple Challenge

Here's a challenge to try right now:

1. Pick one business idea you like from this book.
2. Ask 3 people if they would use it or buy it.
3. Create the simplest version of it you can—just enough to test.
4. Ask for feedback, improve, and try again.

You don't need to wait until next month or next year. You can start this week. Or today.

✓ Final Thought

Being an entrepreneur doesn't mean waiting until you're older.

It means **trying something**, learning from it, and then trying again.

Not everything you do will work. And that's okay.

Because every time you try, you're getting better. Smarter. More confident.

Your business doesn't have to be perfect.

It just has to get started.

So go ahead.

Pick one idea.

Take one step.

The rest will follow.

You've got this.

Final Words from a Fellow Entrepreneur

Hi there—

I'm really glad you made it this far. My name is Gregory Lilien, and I've spent the past 25 years building businesses. I've started over 15 of them—some were big wins, and a few didn't make it. But every single one taught me something that helped me get better.

And here's the truth: **no book, no course, and no adult can fully prepare you for what it's like to build something real.** You just have to start.

I've had my own dad look me straight in the eye and say, "That's a stupid idea."

That idea later turned into something big.

So yeah—**you need to trust your own instincts.**

But you also need to be smart.

Trust Your Hunches—but Always Validate

It's okay to feel excited about an idea. That feeling—that spark—is what starts everything. But you should still go out and **ask people if they actually want it**. Talk to potential customers. Get feedback. Learn what they like and what they don't.

Don't try to prove you're right—try to learn what's true.

You might save yourself weeks (or months) of wasted time.

Spend As Little As Possible to Learn

This one's big: **don't overbuild anything in the beginning.**

I've seen people go into debt because they thought they had to order thousands of units, build fancy websites, or make everything perfect. But what matters most early on is this:

Can you make a simple version of your idea and see if anyone wants it?

That's what we call a **minimum viable product.**

It doesn't have to be pretty. It just has to **work**.

Once people start buying or showing real interest, then you can improve it.

Until then, keep it scrappy.

Don't Just Buy Products — Build Relationships

If you're going to create a physical product and work with a manufacturer or factory, remember this: **you're not just placing an order — you're starting a relationship.**

Factories aren't vending machines. They're teams of people.

If you get to know them — if you're kind, clear, and respectful — they'll often go out of their way to help you. That kind of partnership can save your business one day. It has for me.

Also, a word of caution:

Everyone will tell you to **diversify your supply chain**.

It sounds smart on paper — but it can actually add more problems, especially early on.

You don't need 5 factories. You need one good one.

Don't Overbuy — and Don't Compete on Price Alone

Please don't make the mistake of ordering 1,000 units of something before you've sold even one. **Inventory is one of the easiest ways to lose money fast.** Keep it tight and focused.

And remember: **don't try to be the cheapest option in the market.** That usually ends with you burned out and broke.

Instead, compete on brand. Compete on value. Compete by being different.

Not Everything Has to Be a "Broken Leg Problem"

You've probably heard that good businesses solve problems. That's true.

But not every winning product has to be urgent or life-saving. **Godiva doesn't solve a problem. Neither does a Squishmallow.**

Sometimes people just want to feel good. Be comforted. Be delighted.

You can absolutely build a business around something **fun, beautiful, or just because.**

Make Your Brand Different

This one matters more than you think:

Don't look like everyone else.

Don't use the same fonts, same colors, same packaging style as the brand next to you. **Find your own voice.** Make people feel something when they see your product—even if it's just, "Wow, that's cool."

A great brand gets remembered. A bland one gets ignored.

Think About Pricing More Than Once

Pricing is not "set it and forget it."

You should regularly ask yourself:

- Is my price too low?
- Am I offering too much for too little?
- Is my brand strong enough to raise the price?

Price affects perception.

And perception affects sales. So treat it like a tool—not a guess.

Final Advice from Me to You

You're going to make mistakes. That's part of the game.

You're going to feel stuck sometimes. That's also part of the game.

But if you're honest, stay curious, and show up consistently—you'll keep getting better.

Every great entrepreneur was once where you are right now:

Just someone with an idea, a little courage, and a lot to learn.

So go start something.

Mess it up.

Fix it.

Learn.

Build again.

You've already got more knowledge than I did when I was your age.

And trust me—**you've got this.**

Gregory Lilien

Gregory Lilien

Entrepreneur, Creator, and Proud Mistake-Maker